How to Buy, Sell and

CW00796476

How to Buy, Sell and Own Shares

Published by Consumers' Association
and Hodder and Stoughton

EDITOR
Jane Vass

CONTRIBUTORS
Tim Crawley-Boevey
Jane Vass
Simon Hinde
Anthony Bailey
Virginia Wallis
Simon Richmond
Jonquil Lowe

INDEX COMPILED BY
Pamela Le Gassick

Which? Books are commissioned and researched
by The Association for Consumer Research
and published by Consumers' Association,
2 Marylebone Road, London NW1 4DX and
Hodder & Stoughton, 47 Bedford Square,
London WC1B 3DP

Typographic design by Tim Higgins
Cover illustration by John Holder

First edition 1987
Second edition 1988

**British Library Cataloguing in Publication
Data**
How to buy, sell and own shares: a practical guide for the
private investor — 2nd ed.
1. Great Britain. Stocks & shares — Investment —
Manuals
I. Consumers' Association
332.6'322

ISBN 0 340 49162 0

Typeset by Tradespools Ltd, Frome, Somerset
Printed and bound in Great Britain by Anchor
Brendon Ltd

Contents

Introduction

Over the past ten years, investing in shares could have brought you large rewards. Share prices rose by an average of 15 per cent a year – even taking account of the October 1987 stock market crash. But in the short term, shareholders need to have strong nerves. In October 1987, the value of shares on the London Stock Exchange fell by 22 per cent in one week.

So it's important to buy shares with your eyes open – and this book aims to help you do precisely that. It's divided into four parts:

- **The basics** Chapters 1 to 7 cover all the things a new shareowner or someone thinking about buying shares for the first time should know: exactly what shares are, the mechanics (and the electronics) of buying and selling them, how they might affect your tax bill, and even if you should buy them at all. Looking on the gloomy side, it also tells you what safeguards there are against rogues.
- **Choosing shares** – the difficult bit for any shareholder. We don't come up with any magic nostrums for instant fortune in the stock market – the chances are that if there were any the professionals would have come up with them long ago. But Chapters 8 to 12 explain the ways in which the stock market tends to move; debunk several myths; and tell you how you can find out about the companies you invest in.
- **Owning shares** – or, what to do with them once you've got them. Chapters 13 to 17 tell you how to keep track of your shares, the various 'perks' that might come your way, and what to do if you're faced with a rights or scrip issue, a takeover or a merger.
- **Next steps** So you've been investing in shares for some time now? If you want to go further and explore other ways of investing in shares, and other ways of using them, Chapters 18 and 19 tell you about the Unlisted Securities Market, the Third Market, the Over-the-Counter Market, investing overseas, the Business Expansion Scheme and traded options. The section is rounded off with a Glossary, and a list of useful addresses.

Throughout the text, key words which are explained in the Glossary are printed in **bold**.

Section I

The basics

1 *The changing face of shares*

The 1980s could well be termed the decade when the ordinary saver re-discovered the share. We say re-discovered, because the publicity surrounding the many recent new issues, particularly the government privatisations with their huge advertising campaigns, might lead you to think that this is a new phenomenon. But, in fact, over the past 20 years a higher and higher proportion of shares has moved from private ownership into the hands of institutions such as banks and pension funds. What's happening now is that the number of individuals who own shares has risen dramatically, and it's estimated that more than one in five adults now owns shares. But the underlying investment has remained the same – when you put your hard-earned money into shares, you're investing in the possible success of a particular company. So it's as well to understand why that company might have issued shares in the first place.

Why companies issue shares

The idea of shares grew up in the sixteenth and seventeenth centuries as a way for merchants to pool their money. In that way, the ancestor of the modern-day entrepreneur then had enough capital to undertake large ventures, and also achieved safety in numbers – if a venture failed, the losses were spread out over several merchants. If the venture was successful, they shared the profits too.

The idea hasn't changed that much over the centuries. Today, a company considering 'going public' might also be doing so as a way of raising money in order to grow. A company in this position has two main options: it can borrow the money; or it can issue shares, when the money raised is called 'equity capital' because the company is selling off a share in its value or equity (hence **equities**, a common name for shares).

If a company favours borrowing, it would eventually have to give the money back. If a bank is willing to lend for a reasonably long period (years rather than months) it will probably want 'security' – i.e. a claim on some of the company's assets, such as a factory or land. This in itself can be difficult for companies whose assets are intangible, such as public relations companies. The company could also try to borrow from the general public or from financial institutions by issuing **loan stock** or debentures (loans for a fixed period offering a fixed amount of interest), sometimes secured on some of the company's assets. The table opposite shows some of the different ways in which a company can raise money from the public.

'Going public': the pros ...

Issuing shares can be a useful alternative to borrowing. By asking the general public to finance the company in return for a stake – a 'share' – in the company itself, a long-term source of funds opens up. Ironically, this can also make it easier for the company to raise short-term finance, because the company's standing tends to go up if the bank (and the general public) see that shareholders are prepared to risk their money in it.

There's also a benefit for the original owners of the company. While they are the only owners, their money may be tied up in the company's belongings, such as factories and machinery. They can't sell this sort of thing without disrupting the work of the company, so can't benefit fully from the success of their enterprise. If, on the other hand, they sell off part of the company itself to the public, they can unlock cash from their investment. This is a major reason for the recent spate of government privatisations – i.e. the sales of nationally owned bodies such as British Gas and British Airways. In the 1986–87 tax year alone, these privatisations raised an estimated £4.4 *billion*.

... and the cons

There is a price to pay for 'going public'. The company becomes accountable to its shareholders. The original owners may lose their control over the company's future. If the shareholders' confidence in the company

How a company can raise money

Debentures (loan capital)
The company pays a fixed rate of interest, and there's normally a fixed repayment date. The interest must be paid whether or not the company makes a profit.

Equity capital
In other words, shares. Shareholders have a stake in the company, but whether or not they get any income from it depends on the company's profits. If the company is wound up, shareholders rank below holders of loan stock and debentures in getting their money back.

type of debenture	how they work	type of share	how they work
CONVERT-IBLES	give the holder the option to convert to ordinary shares for a fixed price at one or more fixed dates. They pay a fixed rate of interest	ORDINARY SHARES	entitle the holder to a share in profits after holders of debentures, loan stock and preference shares have been paid. They usually carry voting rights
MORTGAGE-BACKED (OR FIXED)	loan backed up by mortgages on specific company property	PREFER-ENCE SHARES	take preference over ordinary shares in payment of income and return of capital. They usually carry a fixed rate of interest, and have no voting rights
FLOATING	backed up by a 'floating charge', i.e. a mortgage on all the company's assets	'A' SHARES	name often given to shares with different voting rights from ordinary shares – e.g. no voting rights
UNSECURED LOAN STOCK	the most common form of debenture – not backed up by any company property	'B' SHARES	name given to other types of shares, e.g. ones which offer more shares instead of income; usually a lower market price than ordinary shares

wanes, they can sell the shares, causing a fall in the share price – which in turn could make the company vulnerable to takeover by another hungry company on the prowl. The loss of confidence may also make it difficult for the company to raise extra money – either by borrowing or by issuing further shares.

On the other side of the coin, if the company is so popular that huge numbers of people buy small holdings in it, the cost of keeping those shareholders informed, consulting them when necessary, and sending out small cheques for dividends, can mount up. To get round this, the company may issue special types of share, or restrict perks to certain types of share – as European Ferries did in 1984. Demand for their shares grew to such an extent, because of the attractive perks attached, that those perks have been restricted to holders of preference shares.

New shares or old?

If you want to buy shares you have the choice of either buying them new or buying them second-hand. When you buy them as a 'new issue' you pay a price which is either set by the company or as the result of an auctioning process (see Chapter 5 for the mechanics). If you opt to buy second-hand, the price you pay depends on the number of sellers and buyers around – in other words, on supply and demand.

Buying a 'new issue' has the advantage of being the cheaper of the two options. Because you are buying direct from the company you don't have to pay anything to the middlemen, such as commission to a broker. The problem is that with a new issue you don't usually know if you are buying at the 'right' price – which depends purely on what other people are willing to pay for the shares. If the price you eventually pay for the new issue is too high, the issue will flop, and you could be left with shares you can get rid of only for less than you paid for them. Or, if the issue is *too* popular, the issuers may either have to reduce the number of shares each applicant gets, or even decide who gets them by holding a ballot. This could leave you with no shares at all, or so few that the costs of selling them eat up any profits.

Buying second-hand has the advantage that the price you pay is one that depends on the number of people who want to buy and sell that particular share – so the market-place has already set the 'right' price. But buying second-hand will cost you more (other things being equal) because you'll have broker's commission and some tax to pay.

The stock market – a traditional business

Around the basically simple need for companies to find a convenient way to finance their activities, a whole industry has grown up. There are **stockbrokers** to buy and sell on the investor's behalf, **market-makers** to act as wholesalers for lines of stock, and a number of market-places where shares can be traded.

You don't *have* to buy or sell your shares on the stock market. Providing you can find a willing buyer or seller, you can do the deal between yourselves, cutting out the middlemen – we tell you how on page 44. But what if you want to sell 1,000 shares in Industrious Industries, and the only person you can find who's interested wants 500 shares? This is where the stock market comes in. There are market-makers who act as wholesalers, and stockbrokers to make sure you can deal in as many shares as you want, and find you the best price.

Strictly speaking, there's not just one stock market. Stocks and shares can be traded in several different places in this country, and in market-places abroad. The most famous market-place in the United Kingdom, and the oldest, is the Stock Exchange itself. This actually consists of several regional exchanges in places like Manchester, Glasgow and Dublin, as well as the familiar London exchange. These regional exchanges used to be completely separate bodies which came together in federation in 1965, and merged completely in 1973. The Stock Exchange has trading floors in London, Birmingham, Glasgow and Dublin. Here the market-makers can set up their stalls, for the brokers to browse round in search of the best prices. But since the change in working practices known as Big Bang (see below), the market trading floors have almost emptied, as computers remove the need for brokers to leave their offices in search of the best price. In fact the London trading floor is now used only for traded options (see Chapter 19).

'Big Bang' – a new era

Although the reasons why companies need the stock market have changed very little, the stock market itself has undergone an amazing transformation. On 27 October 1986 a series of changes took effect, so wide-reaching that market wags christened it 'Big Bang' (a similar change in America was known as 'Mayday').

What happened on that day was that the Stock Exchange dropped its previous fixed scale of minimum commissions for buying and selling shares, and for the first time allowed the same people to act as both stockbrokers and share wholesalers. The reasons for these changes, and their effects, are wide-reaching.

Before Big Bang, the structure of the Stock Exchange had remained essentially the same for many centuries. Members were divided into:

- **stockbrokers,** who could only buy and sell for their customers, and were forbidden to buy and sell shares on their own behalf, and
- **jobbers,** who could buy and sell lines of stock themselves, but couldn't deal directly with the public – only with the stockbrokers acting as agents for the public.

This system was known as 'single capacity', because each type of member could carry out only one function.

Stockbrokers made their money by charging their customers commission, and the minimum commissions were laid down by the Stock Exchange. In practice this meant that everybody tended to charge the same. Jobbers made their money by selling their shares for more than they paid for them. The difference between the price at which the jobber bought (called the **bid** price) and the price at which the jobber sold (the **offer** price) was known as the 'jobber's turn'.

The need for Big Bang was born in 1983, when the Office of Fair Trading threatened to bring a case against the rule book of the Stock Exchange in the Restrictive Practices Court. To avoid this, the Stock Exchange agreed to drop its scale of minimum commissions and to allow large 'outside' bodies, such as banks, to become members. One reason for this second change was the growth in international trading: unless the existing members could get the increased financial backing to be gained by teaming up with larger financial institutions, the international trade would pass them by, and the United Kingdom Stock Exchange would lose its importance. 'Outside' institutions were allowed to become full members from 1 March 1986.

Big Bang set up a domino effect. The death of minimum commissions led in turn to:

- **The death of the strict distinction between broker and jobber**
  It was argued that competition would force commission rates down. If share prices and dealing costs were to remain competitive – especially with overseas market-places such as Wall Street – there just wouldn't be enough money about to support both jobbers and brokers. The answer was to let one person act in both capacities – a so-called 'dual capacity' system. This means that members of the Stock Exchange are now allowed to act both as agents for customers and to buy and sell shares themselves as 'principals' – i.e. as 'market-makers'

(technically, 'broker-dealers'). But many firms have decided to act only as agents for clients, and they are known as 'agency-brokers'. All these official terms haven't wiped out the term 'stockbroker', however – it is still widely used.

- **Possible conflicts of interest** If the company which is buying shares for you can fill your orders from its own shelves, how do you know you are getting the best price available? To counter this, broker-dealers are required to act only in one of their capacities at *any one time* – so they must act either as your agent or on their own behalf, but not both; all deals are now recorded on computer, so it's easy to go back and check that the deal really was to your best advantage. To counter other possible conflicts of interest, invisible boundaries, known as '**Chinese walls**', separate the parts of a firm which act as agents, and those which act as principals. See Chapter 7 for the other protection available to the shareholder under the Financial Services Act, which has come into force during 1988.

- **New ways of buying and selling shares** New computer systems have grown up to cope with the changes. Instead of walking around the Stock Exchange trading floors to see what prices are on offer, stockbrokers can just tap into their computers. For many shares, computers can display the cheapest price for you automatically – cutting down on possible conflicts of interest.

- **Wide variations in commission rates** Before Big Bang, it was feared that although the abolition of minimum commissions would lead to lower charges for big institutional investors, private investors might have to pay more. On the whole, this has happened. There's a wider range of commission rates, but minimum commission levels (on deals of under £1,200 or so) have risen steeply. If you want advice, you may find it more difficult to get, unless you have a large amount of money to invest, or are willing to pay extra for it. Either way, it's now essential to shop around.

The new shareholder

Government privatisations, increasing share prices over the last decade, tax incentives to buy shares, a new awareness of the stock market as a result of the publicity surrounding Big Bang – all these factors have produced an increase in the number of private shareholders. A *Which?* survey in 1987 found that over half our readers had shares, as opposed to a third in 1982. Should you join them (if you haven't already)?

2 Why buy shares?

The return you hope to get from your shares comes in two forms:

- **Income,** in the form of a regular **dividend**. Usually twice a year, a company will look at its after-tax profits and set a proportion aside as a 'reserve', to finance further growth or help run the business. Anything left over is shared out among the shareholders as a dividend. The amount is announced by the directors, usually as so many pence per share – so if you have 1,000 shares in a company, for example, and the dividend is 4p net per share, your dividend is £40. ('Net' means that your dividend comes with the equivalent of basic-rate tax already paid – so if you are a basic-rate taxpayer there's no more tax to pay.) Then, soon after the annual general meeting, you will be sent a 'dividend warrant' (like a cheque) together with a tax voucher (showing the amount of tax deemed to have been paid). You can, if you wish, ask to have your dividend paid directly to a bank. One dividend, called the 'interim' dividend and usually the smaller of the two, is paid after the announcement of the half-yearly results. The other dividend, called the 'final' dividend, is paid at the end of the company's trading year. However, a company is not obliged to pay any dividend at all to ordinary shareholders – if it is doing badly it could 'pass' the dividend.
- **Growth in the value of your shares** Look at the graph opposite showing the share price of Wheats Beers. If you'd been brave enough to invest in autumn 1985 when shares stood at, say, 42p each, and sold when the share price hit 168p in September 1987, you'd have made a capital gain of 168p−42p=126p a share (though buying and selling costs would have reduced the profit). But if you'd invested in early 1984, when the share price stood at 164p, you would have seen the price *fall* to 42p by autumn 1985 – a capital loss of 122p.

How good a return?

Over the past 10 years investing in shares could have given you a good return. Measured by the **Financial Times-Actuaries All-Share Index**, an original investment of £1,000 in May 1978 could now (May 1988) be worth around £4,300 – and that's not counting the income you'd have received. That's well over the amount your money would have needed to

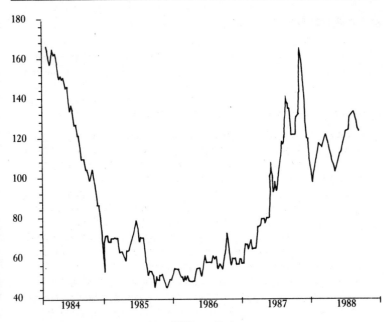

Graph showing the share price of Wheats Beers.

grow to in order to keep up with inflation. If you'd invested the money in a building society, you would have ended up with £1,000 (again, ignoring income) over the same period. **But:**

- these figures are averages only. If you pick the wrong shares, you could end up with considerably less than from stashing the money away in your building society – or even nothing, if the companies you invest in go bankrupt
- these figures ignore short-term blips in the steady upward path of share growth
- these figures reflect a long-term period of steady share growth. At times the stock market as a whole can fall – a **bear market** (see Chapter 8) – as happened in October 1987
- these figures ignore the costs of buying and selling shares.

Should you buy shares?

Shares have the advantage of allowing you to share in the successes (but also the failures) of the companies in which you invest. But before you take the plunge and buy shares, ask yourself the following questions. If the answers to them are no, think again before buying shares. Instead, consider one of the alternative investments suggested below and described in the rest of this chapter.

● Do you have an emergency source of money? You can't regard your shares as a ready source of cash. If you need the money you've got tied up in the stock market, you may be forced to sell your shares when the share price is low.
  If no: *consider no-notice building society or bank accounts, or make sure you can borrow the money.*
● Do you have a mortgage and a pension?
  If no: *You should make sure that your basic finances are sound before embarking on share-buying – and some interest payments on mortgages and pension contributions can be set against your tax bill.*
● Do you have enough to invest? Many stockbrokers set a minimum commission of around £20 to £25 (and often more), so if you want to buy less than around £1,200-worth of shares in one company the costs of buying and selling will eat up a large proportion of your investment. And the risks of losing all your money are higher if you invest in only one company, so you should aim to build up a portfolio of shares in, say, five to ten companies. For these reasons, £6,000 is the very least you should have available before you think of shares – and, preferably, much more.
  If no: *consider unit trusts, investment trust companies, building society and bank high-interest accounts, National Savings, investment-type life insurance.*
● Are your nerves strong enough to live with the risk that the value of your shares could seesaw up and down from day to day? For example, in late March 1987 fears of a trade war with Japan wiped £10 billion off share values overnight – but a month later prices had recovered.
  If no: *consider British Government stocks, National Savings, building society and bank high-interest accounts.*
● Can you give your investment time to recover from this sort of plunge downwards? Because of the daily ups and downs, shares are a long-term investment. If you're going to need to sell your shares at a particular time, forget it.
  If no: *consider British Government stocks maturing when you will need the money, building society and bank high-interest accounts.*

Other ways to invest a lump sum for capital growth

The investments described in this section offer one of the major benefits of shares – the chance of capital growth. But there's usually less risk attached, either because you're pooling the risk with other people, or because you can use them in a way that reduces some of the risks.

Unit trusts

When you buy units in a unit trust fund, you are investing in a 'pool' of different investments held by trustees (often a bank). The trustees hold your money in their name and ensure that the fund is properly run, but they have no say in the investment decisions. The decisions about what to buy and sell are taken by the unit trust company itself, which makes a yearly charge of, say, one per cent of the value of your investment.

The idea is that the total money invested in the fund is spread out over a number of different investments, so that the amount one person pays to have a stake in all the investments can be low – the minimum initial investment in a unit trust can range from £250 to £1,000, and several unit trust companies run schemes for saving smaller amounts regularly.

At the moment, unit trusts can invest only in shares and British Government stocks, though there are proposals to add other types of investments. However, many funds specialise in, say, shares in British companies or small but potentially high-growth companies. Unit trust companies tend to build up 'stables' of funds, so that their investors can choose between a range of more 'risky' funds or a safer, staider, general growth fund of mixed investments.

You can make money from unit trusts in two ways. First, the income the fund gets from the investments it contains is shared out between the unit-holders as a 'distribution', usually twice yearly. Different funds provide varying amounts of income. Secondly, you hope to make a capital gain, so that the value of your units when you sell is greater than the amount you first paid for them. The value of the fund goes up and down in line with the value of the investments it contains.

Buying and selling You can deal direct with the unit trust company, or buy through a bank, investment adviser or stockbroker, who will be earning commission. As with shares, the prices of the units are lower when you are selling (the 'bid' price) than if you are buying (the 'offer' price). This difference, known as the 'bid to offer spread', covers the cost of commission and other buying costs.

How they are taxed The equivalent of basic-rate tax is deducted from the distributions before you get them. You can claim it back if you have paid too much tax (or shouldn't pay tax at all), but if you are a higher-rate taxpayer you will have to pay the taxman extra.

You may have to pay capital gains tax on any capital gain you make when you sell units if your net taxable gains for the year are above a certain limit (£5,000 in 1988–89).

Should you buy? Unit trusts are a useful way of spreading a relatively small amount of money over a number of investments, if you cannot afford the £6,000 minimum you really need to invest in shares direct. Some funds have increased their unit prices by spectacular amounts over the past few years, beating inflation by miles – but some have made their investors a considerable loss. To reduce the risks, choose a general fund, rather than a very specialist one, and buy units in several funds. Remember that you may have to leave your money in the trust for some years to get the full benefit.

Investment trust companies

Strictly speaking, investment trust companies are just companies quoted on the Stock Exchange; the difference is that their business is investing in the shares of other companies. So by buying shares in an investment trust you're spreading your money over a number of companies' shares. This cuts down the amount you need to invest – but there's an extra risk: however valuable the shares in which the trust invests, the trust's share price could still fall if investors decide they don't want to buy its shares (if, for example, they lose faith in its management).

The main difference between a unit trust and an investment trust lies in how the units and shares in each are valued. The price you pay for a unit in a unit trust reflects the value of all the investments in the trust fund. The price you pay for a share in an investment trust may, however, be higher or lower than the value of all its investments (the **net asset value**). Whether the price is higher or lower (in the stock market jargon, stands at a **premium** or a **discount**) depends on the trust's popularity with investors.

As with other companies' shares, you may get dividends from an investment trust, and a chance to make a capital gain (or the risk of making a capital loss).

Buying and selling Exactly the same as for other companies' shares (see Chapter 5), and the share prices are quoted in the newspapers. Because you normally have to use a bank, stockbroker, or other investment adviser, it's usually not worth buying much less than £1,200-worth of shares in one investment trust company. A few companies run regular savings schemes that allow you to invest a small amount each month without going through a broker.

How they are taxed Just like other shares (see Chapter 6).

Should you buy? Investment trust companies are worth considering if you don't have enough money to invest direct in a wide spread of shares. And because their price depends partly on their popularity, they can do extremely well in good times for shares generally (though rather poorly in lean times). But since, unlike unit trusts, investment trust companies can buy some of their investments on credit, the ups and downs in their share prices can be exaggerated. (Though there are proposals to allow unit trusts to borrow money for investment too.) Look at them as a fairly long-term investment.

Single-premium bonds

These are the life insurance industry's answer to the problem of spreading a relatively small lump sum over a number of investments. The money you invest buys you a number of units in one of the insurance company's investment funds. The price you pay for each unit is a share of the value of the investments in the fund. The unit price fluctuates in line with the value of the investments.

So far, bonds sound exactly like unit trusts. But the investment fund doesn't normally pay out an income. If you want to draw an income, you have to cash in a number of units. Obviously, if you want more income than the amount by which the value of the fund grows, you will find yourself eating into the underlying value of the bond.

Insurance funds invest in other things as well as shares and British Government stocks, for example property, and they can hold your money as cash. They can also set up 'managed funds', where the money is moved between different sorts of investment at the discretion of the managers. Once you have bought a bond, you can generally switch your money between all the funds the insurance company runs, either free (e.g. the first switch free each year) or at low cost.

The most important difference between unit trusts and single-premium bonds, is that they are technically life insurance policies – there is a small amount of life insurance cover attached to them (which often amounts only to the value of your investment). It means that they are taxed in a completely different way, and this affects your return.

Buying and selling You can either buy direct from the insurance company or through an insurance or other investment adviser. This won't cost you anything, as the insurance company will pay them commission, but to recoup this and other costs there is an initial charge and an annual management charge. As with unit trusts, the price you get for your units when you sell (the 'bid' price) is lower than the price at which the units can be bought (the 'offer' price).

How they are taxed   With unit trusts, the amount of income tax and capital gains tax you pay depends on your own tax position when you get the income or capital gain from the fund, and the unit trust funds themselves are tax-free. The position is reversed for bonds: the money you draw from the funds is free of basic-rate income tax and capital gains tax, but the funds themselves are taxed. So, in effect, you can't escape paying tax.

When you yourself draw money from the fund, there's no basic-rate income tax to pay. And, providing you don't draw out more than five per cent a year of your original investment, any higher-rate tax bill is put off until you finally cash in the bond. It is payable at your tax rates then (by which time you might be a basic-rate taxpayer anyway). Higher-rate taxpayers can also claim 'top-slicing' relief, which can reduce the amount of any higher-rate tax due.

Should you buy?   Because of the different tax treatment, a single-premium bond will usually produce a lower return than a unit trust investing in exactly the same things. However, bonds might be worth considering if you want to invest in a wide range of investments, and want to be able to switch between different funds quickly and cheaply, or if you're worried about your money going into shares (because you fear a stock market crash). They are also useful for higher-rate taxpayers who have used up their capital gains tax allowance, and who want to put off any income tax till later.

British Government stocks (gilts)
When you buy gilts, you're lending your money to the government, usually for a fixed period of time and for a fixed amount of interest. In that respect they're rather like buying loan stock in an ordinary company, but much more secure since the government is unlikely ever to default on its loans.

Also like company shares, you can buy gilts either new or second-hand. Either way, the price is quoted for each £100 'nominal' of gilts. The 'nominal' value is rather like the face value of an antique coin: the price you actually have to pay for the gilt may be higher or lower (you don't have to buy the gilt in £100 lots).

After the end of the fixed period of time for which the gilt lasts, it is 'redeemed' and you get back £100 for each £100 nominal you hold. So if you hold the gilt until it is redeemed, you get a return which is fixed and guaranteed from the time that you buy. In the meantime you get a fixed rate of interest, usually half-yearly, which can be as low as two per cent or as high as fourteen per cent, depending on the gilt. The interest rate is called the 'coupon'.

There is a huge array of gilts on offer, listed in most daily newspapers under 'British funds'. Their names tell you what they offer: for example, *Treasury 10½% 2005* pays out a yearly income before tax of £10.50 for every £100 nominal of stock, and will be redeemed in the year 2005, when you will get £100 for each £100 nominal you hold (the word 'Treasury' doesn't tell you anything). Before redemption, you can buy and sell the gilt for a price which varies with supply and demand: for example, it could be £95 per £100 nominal, or £105, depending on factors such as how long the gilt has to run, and interest rates in general. Gilts prices tend to rise when interest rates fall, because the fixed income they offer starts to look more attractive to investors, and vice versa.

There are other types of gilts: the main alternative is index-linked gilts. With these, both the coupon and the nominal value are linked to the Retail Prices Index. There are also 'convertible' gilts which can be exchanged at a set time in the future for some other gilt – e.g. one with a longer time until redemption. A few gilts are 'undated', with no set redemption date: there are also a few gilts with variable interest rates.

Buying and selling You can buy new issues through advertisements in daily newspapers. New issues have the advantage that there is no commission or other charge for buying them.

Second-hand gilts can be bought and sold on the Stock Exchange, in which case you will need to use a stockbroker, bank, or other investment adviser, and will have to pay commission varying between 0.25 per cent and 1 per cent of the cost. Minimum commissions like those for share dealing will put up the cost for small investors. Instead, you can buy through your post office, or by post, if you use the National Savings Stock Register. Here the charges are £1 for buying or selling each £250 of stock, or part of £250, with a lower charge of 10p per £10 if selling less than £100 of stock. However, because of the time delay in dealing by post, you can't be sure exactly what the price is going to be.

How they are taxed Similar to shares – basic-rate income tax is usually deducted from the income before it is paid to you. (Though if you buy through the National Savings Stock Register, the income is paid gross.) Non-taxpayers may be able to reclaim tax: higher-rate taxpayers will have to pay extra. But unlike gains on shares, any gains you make on disposing of a gilt after 1 July 1986 are free of capital gains tax.

Should you buy? Gilts are a versatile home for your money, and because of their underlying security your initial investment can be smaller than the amount needed for shares (a minimum of around £1,000 is sensible). If you are prepared to hang on to your gilts until redemption they offer a secure return and a regular fixed income, or you can sell before redemption in the hope of making a capital gain.

The wide range of gilts available means that you can choose how long you want to invest for, and people who want a high income, and non-taxpayers, can choose 'high coupon' gilts (those with a high interest rate). If you're more interested in capital growth, or are a higher-rate taxpayer, choose 'low coupon' gilts – because more of the return comes in the form of tax-free capital gains, whereas income is taxed at up to 40 per cent. Index-linked gilts offer the chance for your money to keep up with inflation.

3 Getting into shares

You can take the plunge by buying direct. Or should you dip a toe in the water first, by buying shares through a Personal Equity Plan (PEP) or in your employer's company?

Buying direct

This has the advantage of giving you the widest scope, and allowing you to spread your share-buying over a wide range of companies. On the other hand, you're on your own when it comes to deciding what to buy and sell. Chapter 9 describes how the stock market pigeon-holes shares into different types, but the most basic distinction between companies is by the market-place on which their shares are traded.

Over 2,600 UK companies have met stringent conditions in order to get a full Stock Exchange listing. Among these conditions are requirements that:

- The company must have at least 25 per cent of its shares in the hands of the public (so that there's a reasonable certainty that the shares can always be traded).
- It must have at least five years' trading record (so that by the time it comes to the market it should be fairly well established).
- The company must have a 'market capitalisation' of at least £700,000 (this is the company's price tag – in other words, the total market value of all the ordinary shares issued).
- The company must abide by a number of rules about the disclosure of information, including the requirement to send shareholders copies of the company's annual report and accounts.
- The directors must abide by a code of dealing.

The attraction of a full listing for a company is that it improves its standing with the public and with the bank manager. But the Stock Exchange also runs two subsidiary markets for companies that can't, or won't, meet such stringent conditions – the **Unlisted Securities Market**, started in November 1980, and the baby of the three, the **Third Market**, with fewer conditions, started in January 1987.

Totally separate from the Stock Exchange market-places is the **Over-**

the-Counter Market. There are no conditions for companies wishing to have their shares traded here. And, until the Financial Services Act comes into full effect during 1988, there is little protection from rogue salesmen.

Which market-place for your money?

There's more about the Unlisted Securities Market, the Third Market, and the Over-the-Counter Market in Chapter 18. But we'd advise the novice share-buyer to steer clear. The shares traded on them tend to be in smaller companies, and may be less actively traded – in other words, bought and sold less frequently. So you may find it difficult to get rid of your shares. By contrast, companies with a full Stock Exchange listing are usually well established and actively traded – though this is no guarantee that they won't turn out to be poor investments!

Buying through a Personal Equity Plan (PEP)

PEPs were introduced in January 1987. Their main attraction is that they allow you to invest a maximum of £3,000 a year in shares and other share-related investments without paying tax on the dividend income or on any capital gain you may make when you come to sell. Also, because they are aimed at the novice investor who may have become increasingly aware of the advantages of stock market investment through government privatisations, the rules were designed to make owning shares through a PEP relatively simple from the investor's point of view. But PEPs can be an expensive option.

The prime restriction is that you can invest in a PEP only through a 'plan manager', who may be a bank, building society, unit trust manager or other investment adviser authorised to deal in shares. The plan manager takes care of all the paperwork for you – buying shares on your behalf and registering your name with the company in whom you have bought shares. They can arrange to send you the annual report and accounts of the company, and for you to go to its annual general meeting if you wish – but these things can cost extra. The plan manager also has to reclaim the tax on your share dividends for you, and give the Inland Revenue the necessary details about your investment. You don't usually have to worry about telling the taxman on your tax return.

All you have to do is pick your shares – the rules say that the plan manager must get you the best possible price he can. This may seem little different from buying shares direct – the range of investments you can choose from is very wide. The regulations for PEPs 'limit' PEP investment to shares traded on the Stock Exchange (including the

Unlisted Securities Market), unit trusts and shares in investment trust companies (although these latter two categories are restricted to 25 per cent of your total PEP investment or £540, whichever is larger).

In practice, however, plan managers have limited the kind of shares you can buy, partly because they don't want to see novice investors burning their fingers on risky investments and partly because restricting the choice means they can buy in bulk, which is cheaper. Some PEP schemes (called 'managed' schemes) work very much like unit trusts (see page 19) and all the decisions are taken for you. Other PEPs (called 'non-discretionary' PEPs) let you choose your shares yourself – up to a point. The most widely available non-discretionary PEPs (mainly those from the high-street banks) tend to restrict the shares you can buy to the safe and solid **alpha stocks** (see page 37) although, of course, no share is completely risk free. If you want to choose shares that fall outside the plan manager's restrictions, you may have to pay more for the pleasure.

The costs

From the point of view of convenience, PEPs look very attractive, but because of all the administration a plan manager has to do, even a cheap non-discretionary PEP could cost you upwards of £100 in the first year on an investment of £3,000. And that's if you choose your shares and stick with them – if you want to trade actively, it could cost even more. The charges are generally made up of setting-up fees, dealing charges when you buy and sell (quite good value in most cases and cheaper than buying shares direct), annual administration charges, and sometimes a charge of around £25 for extra services such as arranging for you to attend a company's annual general meeting.

Length of investment

To get the tax advantages, you have to keep your money in your PEP for at least a full calendar year (i.e. 1 January to 31 December – see diagram on page 28). If you don't, your investment is taxed in the normal way. After 31 December of the year in which you start your PEP, you can put no more money into it (although you can start another PEP). After that date, the investments in your PEP can be bought and sold, but the proceeds must be re-invested in the plan until the end of the full calendar year, otherwise you lose the tax advantages.

Should you buy a PEP?

If you've decided that you want to get into shares as a long-term investment, and you don't have the money to build up a balanced portfolio by buying shares direct, a PEP could be a good way of starting off. As well

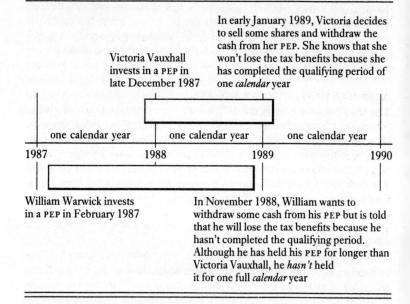

In early January 1989, Victoria decides to sell some shares and withdraw the cash from her PEP. She knows that she won't lose the tax benefits because she has completed the qualifying period of one *calendar* year

Victoria Vauxhall invests in a PEP in late December 1987

one calendar year | one calendar year | one calendar year

1987   1988   1989   1990

William Warwick invests in a PEP in February 1987

In November 1988, William wants to withdraw some cash from his PEP but is told that he will lose the tax benefits because he hasn't completed the qualifying period. Although he has held his PEP for longer than Victoria Vauxhall, he *hasn't* held it for one full *calendar* year

as giving you tax advantages, buying shares through a non-discretionary PEP can provide a sort of half-way house between having to make your own investment decisions and investing in a managed fund in whose investment decisions you have very little involvement.

But you have to be prepared to put up with high charges initially in exchange for having some of the grind taken out of owning shares. The tax benefits will really be worth having only if you keep your shares for five years or more, as in the first years they will probably be swallowed up by the charges. In spite of the government's original intention of encouraging the novice investor, PEPs look most attractive for higher-rate taxpayers and people who have already reached the capital gains tax limit of £5,000.

Buying through your employer's share scheme

Several employers, including household names such as Cadbury Schweppes, Marks & Spencer and Tarmac, have encouraged their workforce to have a stake in the companies by setting up an employee share scheme. There are two basic forms. In profit-sharing schemes the employees are given the shares themselves. In share-option schemes they are given the 'option' to buy the shares at a set price (the 'option' price) at a set date in the future – so if the share price rises beyond the option price they can buy the shares at a discount; if the share price falls below the option price they don't have to buy and they lose nothing.

Since 1978, the government has introduced legislation giving favourable tax treatment to three types of 'approved' employer's share scheme (and most schemes are now approved).

Approved profit-sharing schemes

The least common type in the UK, usually found only in large companies (although it is very popular in the United States). The scheme must be open to all employees with at least five years' service with the company. Each year the company decides how much of its profits it is going to set aside to buy shares for its employees, and puts the money in a special trust. The trustees allocate the shares to the employees – how many depends on things like the employee's age, time with the company, and salary – but for the scheme to be approved the most each employee can get is shares with an initial value of £1,250 (or 10 per cent of earnings if higher), with an overall limit of £5,000-worth of shares. There's no tax to pay when the shares are allocated.

You can't sell the shares for two years (unless you leave on retirement, redundancy, injury or disability). After two years you can sell your shares, either on the open market or (sometimes) back to the trust, but the value of the shares is only free of income tax if you keep them for five years. However, you still have to pay income tax on any dividends you get from them, and any capital gain you make on the original value when you acquired them is liable to capital gains tax (see Chapter 6 for whether you are likely to have to pay this).

SAYE share-option schemes

These are share-option schemes linked to a savings plan, which must be open to all employees with at least five years' service. You agree to pay a fixed sum each month (minimum £10, maximum £100) into a building society or National Savings Save-As-You-Earn (SAYE) plan, for a savings period of five (sometimes seven) years. At the end of this time you get a bonus. When you start the scheme, your company gives you an option to use the money from the SAYE plan to buy its shares at a favourable price – usually 90 per cent of the market value when you started saving.

At the end of the savings period, you have three choices:

- You can exercise your option and buy shares with the money from the SAYE plan at the option price. This will give you a profit if the share price has risen beyond the option price.
- You can choose not to exercise your option, and just take the cash from the SAYE plan.

- If the original savings plan ran for five years, you can choose to leave your money in it for a further two years for another bonus – but you lose the right to exercise your option.

There's no income tax to pay, either when you are given the option or when you get the shares. But there could be capital gains tax to pay when you sell the shares, based on the difference between the price when you bought them and the price when you sold.

Approved share-option schemes

A company doesn't have to offer these options to all its employees. If you are one of the lucky ones, you are allocated options over a set number of shares usually depending on your salary (occasionally on your performance too). You won't have to pay any tax when you are given or use your option, providing that you exercise the option at some time between three and ten years after it is made, and providing you exercise it only at three-yearly intervals. As long as you fulfil these conditions, the only tax you may be liable to is capital gains tax when you finally sell the shares.

Are these schemes worth joining?

Employee share schemes aren't really comparable to investing in the stock market direct. At their best they can give you an excellent profit at no cost to yourself. But before you join one, remember that you're tying both your earnings and your savings to one company's success. Ask yourself the following questions:

- Will you be able to sell the shares? If you work for a private company, or one in difficulties, you may be left with shares you can't sell.
- How much do you have to contribute yourself? With an SAYE share-option scheme, can you commit yourself to a regular saving for five years?
- What happens to your rights under the scheme if you leave your company?
- How much risk is there? With profit-sharing schemes, the value of your shares is affected by ups and downs in the share price – but you can't sell them unless you've had them for two years. So don't count on the shares to pay for essentials.
- Will you have to give up salary or other benefits? If you will, consider whether you prefer the extra risk (and possibility of extra reward) of having a stake in the company's performance, or the security of a regular income.

4 *Who to buy through*

Where to go for advice

It is not possible to drop into a Sharebuyers' Advice Bureau for an unbiased discussion about whether you should buy shares, in which companies, how much you should invest, who you should buy through, and how you should set about it. There are people who will give individual advice – such as stockbrokers – but they are not the right people to start your search with. Such advice is not available as a service on its own, but only as part of a share-dealing package. Always bear in mind that, at the end of the day, the interest of the firm you deal through lies in earning commission from the business you bring, or in making a profit on dealing in the shares they sell you or buy from you – and not in dispensing unbiased information with your best interest as the only aim in view.

There is, however, plenty of published information: in books, financial magazines, and the financial pages of newspapers. Would-be investors in shares – and people who already are investors but have doubts about whether they should be – should start by reading up the subject: hence this book (and other layman's guides to the stock market). Of course, however much homework you do, you may well find that you still do not have the answers to your particular questions. But this is the point at which you *can* sensibly get advice from a stockbroker – either directly or via a bank or building society – since you are by now in a position to make some sort of judgement about the quality of advice you're given.

So when choosing who to deal through (see the section below) take account of the amount of advice you think you are going to need, and the ability – and willingness – of the firm to provide it.

Who to deal through

For most people the choice will be between dealing direct with a stockbroker and dealing with a bank or building society – who will, in turn, deal through a stockbroker. Whether you opt for dealing direct or not will depend on how much you have to invest, and how much advice you are likely to need. Here we outline the main ways to buy.

Stockbrokers

Stockbrokers are members of the Stock Exchange. Strictly speaking, they are now called broker-dealers – some have become **market-makers** or dealers, as well as being brokers. (A broker is someone who acts as your agent in buying and selling shares; a dealer deals in shares on his own account and earns money by making a profit on buying and selling shares.) Until October 1986, stockbrokers were not allowed to be dealers on their own behalf as well (see page 14).

Using a stockbroker direct is likely to be your best choice if you want to:

● get a feel for the share market
● be able to ask for information
● try to ensure that your instructions are understood and acted on with a minimum of delay.

This is especially the case if you're likely to want to do a lot of dealing, and if you have large sums of money to invest. See page 35 for advice on how to choose a stockbroker.

Banks and building societies

Most high-street banks and a growing number of building societies have a share-buying service. The business will be put through a stockbroker; if you want advice, the bank or building society will be able to get it for you from the stockbroker and pass it on. A bank will sometimes use a firm of stockbrokers owned by the bank itself. If you don't feel ready to go into the business of having your own stockbroker, and don't expect to be buying and selling very often, try using a bank or building society. For advice on choosing one, see page 36.

Solicitors and accountants

Like banks and building societies, solicitors and accountants will often arrange to buy and sell shares for you, through a stockbroker. The solicitor or accountant may get a share of the stockbroker's commission; he may also charge a fee. When the commission is to be shared between broker and solicitor/accountant, the stockbroker will sometimes charge a higher-than-normal rate (the *divisible* scale). Your solicitor or accountant has to tell you how much the commission is; solicitors have to pay their share to you (usually via a reduction in their fees) unless you agree that they should keep it.

Other share dealers

There are other share dealers who aren't members of the Stock Exchange, although under the Financial Services Act they must be 'authorised' (see Chapter 7). Before the Financial Services Act came into force, they had to be licensed to sell shares by the Department of Trade and Industry and were therefore known as 'licensed dealers in securities'.

Share dealers run the Over-The-Counter (OTC) Market (see Chapter 18). They may seem more approachable than a stockbroker. But don't be misled by apparently low charges. The 'no-commission' terms that some of them may offer doesn't mean the service is free: they will be taking their fee from the share price (either by charging an over-the-odds price for the shares to a buyer, or by paying less than the going price to the seller).

In the past, some investors have lost money invested through such dealers (and there have been some recent failures). However, authorised share dealers are now covered by the compensation scheme set up under the Financial Services Act.

Share shops

The idea of being able to pop in for advice about investments and/or to buy or sell shares while you're out doing other kinds of shopping sounds appealing. So far, however, there are only a handful of share shops in this country. They may be separate high-street shops, or within large department stores, and are run by stockbrokers. You might find this a more convenient and less impersonal way of dealing in shares than using a stockbroker by phone or using some other intermediary. If so, and you've checked that you aren't paying over the odds for the service, fine.

Prestel

A few stockbrokers provide share information to their clients via Prestel or Prestel CitiService – and may provide a dealing service too. A lot of up-to-the-moment facts can then become available to you on a TV screen or monitor at your home (but no individual advice, of course), and you can put in orders to buy or sell shares at any time of day or night. The costs of dealing will depend on the stockbroker. You can pay extra for the CitiService SEAQ Gateway, and you can then receive SEAQ prices (see page 37). None of this comes cheap. For non-business users, Prestel and Prestel CitiService costs a basic £32 a year, and CitiService SEAQ Gateway an extra £168 a year. But that is before you start paying for information you receive: share price information from CitiService SEAQ Gateway costs 24p per minute. And with all Prestel services there is also a basic time charge (if in working hours), as well as the extra phone bill.

The services you can get

Whether you deal with a stockbroker direct, or through an intermediary like a bank or solicitor, you will have to decide how much you want them to do for you. You may be offered a choice of up to four levels of service. You'll need to think about which of these services you want before you decide who to deal through, and to bear it in mind when you're checking on commission rates, minimum charges and the like. The four levels are as follows:

1 Dealing-only Officially known as **execution-only**, this service is just buying and selling shares on your behalf, with no frills and no advice. With a few brokers, this is the only service you can get. Where you are offered a choice between dealing-only and dealing with advice (see below), dealing-only will be cheaper.

2 Dealing with advice This is the traditional dealing service, often with extra services thrown in (things like regular valuations of your investments and/or an investment newsletter). The individual advice you get with this service is time-consuming and therefore expensive to provide, so expect to pay more than for dealing-only. What you won't get is portfolio management.

3 Advisory or 'non-discretionary' portfolio management With this service, all your share investments are looked after for you, and you get advice from time to time on changes the firm thinks you should make, or on where to make new investments. Unlike discretionary management (below), this service leaves the final decisions to you. Most firms won't provide this service unless your portfolio is worth a certain minimum amount – usually £10,000 to £50,000, but it can be up to £100,000 or even more. There is usually an extra yearly charge on top of the normal share dealing costs for this service.

4 Discretionary portfolio management Here you hand over all the decision-making to the firm doing your portfolio management: they manage your investments and take all the buying and selling decisions for you. From their point of view, this is a lot less troublesome than advisory management; minimum portfolio size is sometimes less and there may not be a yearly charge on top of the share dealing costs.

There may be other services on offer – portfolio management where the investments are in unit trusts, for instance. Again, check charges and shop around.

Choosing a stockbroker

To start with, you need a list of stockbrokers who are willing to take on new private clients. One source is Consumers' Association's publication *Buying, selling and owning shares – an Action Kit from Which?*; another is the Stock Exchange booklet *An introduction to the stock market*. Then, look through the list and pick out three or four brokers that would seem to suit you – on the basis of services offered, charges, any recommendations from friends, and where they are. You will find that there can be significant differences in charges between one stockbroker and another, and between one service and another. For an idea of the range of typical charges, see the Table on this page.

As you can see from the Table, both your choice of stockbroker and your decision about which level of service (see page 34) can make a big difference to the amount you pay in charges, especially if you're dealing often and investing large sums of money at a time.

But shopping around doesn't stop there. Unless all your share deals are for amounts of, say, £1,200 to £1,500 or so, minimum commission charges will matter to you too.

For example, many stockbrokers apply a minimum charge of £20 to £25. If the rate of commission is 1.65 per cent, which is often the case, this means that any deal under £1,515 will incur the £25 minimum – making the commission on small deals relatively expensive. Depending on the stockbroker, minimum charges can go down to £15 or even less – though this is rare – and, particularly with the larger London stockbrokers, can go as high as £40, £50, or even more. Minimum commissions are sometimes much less for sales of small lots of shares.

Examples of stockbrokers' commission charges
(including VAT)

	to buy £1,000-worth of shares		to buy £10,000-worth of shares	
	CHEAPER	PRICIER	CHEAPER	PRICIER
Dealing + advice	£18.98	£57.50	£115	£189.75
Dealing-only	£17.25	£51.75	£75.90	£150.08

Charges are not the only thing to bear in mind when choosing a broker: should you go for a local firm or one of the big London firms? A local firm or branch may be more likely to welcome the small investor, and you may get the benefit of more of their time and attention. A large London firm is unlikely to show much interest unless you have it in mind to invest something like £50,000 or even £100,000. If you do have such large sums to invest, what a big London firm can offer is more technology, on-the-spot information and research back-up.

Once you've chosen a firm (or made a shortlist), make contact with them. Tell them how much dealing you expect to do, and what level of service you want. Ask to speak to (or, even better, see) the person who would be handling your deals, and ask questions. Don't forget that the broker isn't bound to accept your business. He'll probably try to assess whether your business will be worth his while, ask for a bank reference, and make other enquiries about you (in particular, to check that you have not defaulted on payments to another stockbroker). And you are likely to be asked to sign a *Customer agreement* (see Chapter 7).

How to choose a bank or building society

If you have opted to buy and sell shares through a bank or building society rather than direct from a stockbroker, you're probably not dealing in enormous sums of money, so your main concern is avoiding paying charges that are way out of line for small deals. It's worth shopping around a bit, though: charges do vary from bank to bank and building society to building society. And be aware, too, that there may well be administration fees and handling charges to pay on top of the normal commission charges, which can bump up the overall cost of your share deals. Some banks and societies will only accept people who are customers already; unless the total costs work out over the odds, start with your local branch.

5 The mechanics of buying and selling

How shares are bought and sold

Whether you deal directly with a stockbroker to buy and sell shares, or you go through your bank, say, the procedure is essentially the same – it's just that the bank passes your instructions to and from the stockbroker on your behalf.

The newly computerised stockbroker makes deals not face to face with a dealer, but via a VDU screen. He sits surrounded by phones and keyboards and computer screens. When you phone through to buy or sell, he can call up instantly a vast amount of information. Some of this is 'in-house' data – your portfolio, for instance, if that's held by the firm, or information on various companies covered by the firm's analysts. But the dealing system itself is common to all firms of stockbrokers.

The electronic dealing system

Teletext Output of Price Information by Computer (TOPIC) is the Stock Exchange's screen-based price and financial information system. But, most importantly, it is likely to bring to your stockbroker the Stock Exchange Automated Quotation System (SEAQ). This is the computer system which carries price information for many of the shares you might want a stockbroker to deal in for you, and records deals made.

The shares about which information is held on these computerised systems are split into:

- **alpha stocks** – shares of some 100 of the largest and most actively traded companies (and dealings in these make up about two-thirds of all the business of the Stock Exchange)
- **beta stocks** – shares of a further 600 or so companies, the next down from alpha stock firms
- **gamma stocks** – moving down again, the next 1,700 or so companies
- **delta stocks** – the remaining, and least actively traded companies that still have a full Stock Exchange listing.

The information itself differs in detail:

- **For alpha and beta stocks** the SEAQ system shows bid and offer prices. The *bid* price is what you would get if you were selling the shares; the *offer* price is almost always higher, and is what you would have to pay if you wanted to buy the shares. For each alpha stock, prices are quoted by an average of 16 market-makers (fewer for beta stocks). The prices for alpha and beta stocks are 'firm', which means that a market-maker will buy and sell at the price he quotes (prices are based on lots of 1,000 shares, though you can often buy or sell smaller quantities at the same price).

- **For gamma stocks** the SEAQ system quotes 'indicative' prices only. This is meant to be used as a guide, but isn't a firm price.
- **For delta stocks** the broker has to use the TOPIC system. This gives a guide to middle-market prices (which are half way between what a buyer would pay and a seller would get).

Dealing in the 'electronic' market

The broker's job is to do the best he possibly can for his client by tracking down the most favourable price – the highest bid or lowest offer price, depending on whether you're buying or selling. He is bound by the *best execution* rule (see Chapter 7), and must not be influenced by the fact that one of the market-makers indicated on SEAQ when he calls up a particular share may be his own firm.

In fact, for alpha and beta stocks, the SEAQ system helps him to abide by this rule, by picking out highest bid and lowest offer prices – and the firms offering them – at the top of the screen.

At the moment, to conclude the deal the broker has to do the actual buying and selling (at the price displayed on the screen) by direct phone line to the market-makers. SAEF – a development of SEAQ, and standing for SEAQ Automatic Execution Facility – will eliminate all this and mean that the broker can simply press a few more buttons on his computer and the deal will be done automatically at the best price.

The computerisation doesn't stop with the conclusion of the deal, either. Details of all deals go into a computerised settlement system called **TALISMAN** (Transfer Accounting Lodgement for Investors, Stock MANagement for Jobbers). This sorts out what the different broker-dealers owe each other as well as details such as to whom the next dividend on a particular share should be paid.

Share certificates, too, should be computerised by autumn 1989 – and will mean that after then you won't actually get a certificate at all unless you ask for one. Instead, all details of share ownership will be held in a computer system called **TAURUS** (Transfer and AUtomated Registration of Uncertificated Stock).

How to buy shares – a step-by-step guide

Step 1: Decide what and when you want to buy

You're attracted to shares in Bloggs and Bloggs plc, so you check the price in the paper. Yesterday's closing price is shown as 406p. Since there's only one price listed it's likely to be a middle-market one, which means you'd have had to pay a few pence more to buy (and a seller would have got a few pence less). Some papers show closing bid and offer prices instead. Using this price as a rough guide to what you may have to pay, you decide you'd like to buy 400 shares.

Step 2: Buying 'at best'

Phone up your stockbroker and ask for the current offer price of Bloggs and Bloggs plc. It's an alpha stock and your broker will consult the SEAQ screen and give you the information straight away. You're not alone in your interest in Bloggs and Bloggs, and the price has gone up to 418p. If you're happy about this, tell the broker to buy for you 'at best' – i.e. at the best price he can, which should be at or very close to 418p. The best, or 'touch' price is picked out on the SEAQ screen.

Ask the dealer to repeat back to you your instructions and be sure you're happy with them. Once you've given him the go-ahead, you're committed. Not only will the traditional 'My word is my bond' apply – but the transaction has probably been tape-recorded, too.

Step 3: You could set a limit

If Bloggs and Bloggs plc had shot up overnight to a price that seemed just too high to you – 440p, say – you might not want to tell the broker to buy 'at best'. Instead you could give him your order to buy subject to a price limit – 430p, say. Then if the price were to come down to this later, the broker could go ahead immediately and buy for you. He's in a much better position than you, of course, to keep minute-by-minute tabs on the market. Brokers often won't accept a price limit if it's unrealistic. You can set a time limit either for 'immediate execution' (or for trading on that day) or 'for this account only' (i.e. until the end of the current 'account': one of the two-week periods into which the Stock Exchange year divides – see overleaf). Brokers prefer the former type of time limit.

You can ask the broker to ring you back once he's done the deal. Generally, however, you'll hear no more until you get the **contract note** (see overleaf). Of course, if the time limit set has lapsed before the price has come down to your price limit, the deal won't be done at all.

Step 4: Check the contract note carefully
A few days after you've bought your shares, you should get a contract note from the broker. This will confirm:

● how many shares you've bought
● at what price they were bought
● what they cost (called the *consideration* i.e. number of shares × price per share)
● charges on top of the purchase price (see opposite)
● when you must pay by (the next **settlement day** – see Step 5, below).

All contract notes must be time-stamped, or say that the information is available. This makes it possible to check the price you paid against the actual share price prevailing at that time. Check also for delay between the time you gave your order and the time the deal was done. If you spot any discrepancy on the contract note, tell your broker at once. Keep your contract note safe.

Step 5: Paying for your shares
The Stock Exchange works in periods called 'accounts'. Each account normally lasts 10 working days, starting on a Monday and ending on the Friday of the following week. At the end of each account, each investor's purchases and sales of shares are totted up, and the balance becomes due from him on 'settlement day'.

Settlement day is usually the Monday which falls six working days after the final day of the account (i.e. not the following week, but the Monday beginning the week after that). You should send off your cheque in good time to reach the broker by settlement day.

Step 6: Getting your share certificate
Until the whole system of the registration of share ownership is computerised in 1989, your share certificate is the only proof you have of ownership. It should arrive a few weeks (sometimes longer) after the shares have been paid for. When you get it, keep it in a safe place. If it doesn't arrive, contact your broker.

How to sell shares

Steps 1 to 3: Making the deal
You sell shares in essentially the same way that you buy them – by contacting a broker and getting him to deal for you at a price you're happy with (or, at least, prepared to accept). This time, though, the figure the broker looks for on the SEAQ screen is the highest bid price. You don't

have to sell all the shares you own in any one company at the same time – you can sell just some of them.

Step 4: Checking the paperwork

As well as sending you a contract note, the broker sends you a **transfer form**. You sign this and send it back to the broker with your share certificate. (Send the certificate even if you're not selling all your shareholding – you'll get a new one for the shares you're keeping.) Don't delay returning this. Until he's got the share certificate the broker doesn't have to pay you – although many will.

Step 5: Getting paid for your shares

As with buying, getting paid revolves around 'settlement' day. On that day, or the day after, you should get your cheque. If not, chase your broker.

Step 6: Getting your share certificate

If you've sold only part of your shareholding, you should receive a new certificate (called a balance certificate) a few weeks after the deal has gone through.

What it costs to buy and sell shares

The contract note you receive from the stockbroker will set out exactly how much is due to be paid by you or to you on settlement day. If you have made several deals during the same account, the stockbroker's statement sent to you will show the net amount due to you (or from you), taking all the deals together.

In most cases, by far the largest sum will be the 'consideration' – the actual price of the shares. But it's important not to underestimate the other costs involved. These costs can put up the final bill considerably (see Example on page 43) and are made up of:

Stockbroker's commission   This varies from firm to firm, from transaction to transaction (depending on the amount of money involved), and on the sort of service you're getting. If your broker is simply dealing for you, for instance, you could pay a lower rate of commission than if you're getting advice from him. Watch out too for minimum commission charges – often £20 or £25, which can put up the overall cost of buying or selling small or cheap lots of shares considerably.

Before you commit yourself to any particular broking firms, check what their charges are. And don't be diffident about shopping around.

Expect to pay: 1 per cent to 1.65 per cent of the price of the shares (going down to 0.5 per cent on really large deals).

VAT In most cases you have to pay VAT on the stockbroker's commission or on the minimum or maximum charges, depending on what applies to your deal. The only time you'll get away without paying VAT is if the stockbroker combines dealing and market-making in the same firm *and* has bought your shares from, or sold them to, his own firm. Most firms, though, are operating their broking and market-making sides as two separate companies.

Expect to pay: VAT at the current rate (15 per cent at the moment).

Stamp Duty Only buyers of shares pay this. It's the one charge you avoid if you're a seller. There is pressure on the Chancellor of the Exchequer to abolish Stamp Duty on share transactions every year when the Budget approaches. Until he does, you'll continue to pay this on the consideration – the actual cost of the shares – but not on the other charges.

Expect to pay: 0.5 per cent of the cost of the shares, rounded up to the nearest 50p, payable only if you're buying, not if you're selling.

Contract levy There's a levy of 80p on all transactions over £1,000, buying or selling. Part of this goes towards financing the Panel on Takeovers and Mergers, one of the regulatory bodies overseeing the functioning of the stock market. And part goes towards the fees which the Stock Exchange and The Securities Association have to pay to the Securities and Investments Board. It therefore represents part – though only a small part – of the cost of regulation and investor protection provided by the Financial Services Act.

Expect to pay: 80p on all transactions over £1,000.

And a hidden cost...

All the charges shown above will appear on the contract note you get from the broker. While you shouldn't underestimate the difference these dealing costs can make to the profitability – or not – of a purchase, there's a further hidden charge which can be the biggest of all. At any one time, there's a gap between the offer price at which you'd buy a share, and the (lower) bid price you'd get if you were selling. You should take this into account as a charge on you – since it can make quite a difference to the potential profits you make from your share dealing. While it's generally around one or two per cent (or even less for really fast-moving popular shares) it can be as much as ten per cent or even more on unpopular stocks. The offer price may also be higher and the bid price lower – and therefore the gap greater – if you're dealing in very small numbers of shares. The example opposite demonstrates the difference this (and the other costs involved) can make to your 'profits'.

Buying and selling costs

Why you may need an eight per cent rise in the share price just to break even

buying 250 shares in Bloggs and Bloggs plc

Consideration: 250 Bloggs and Bloggs plc at 418p	£1,045.00
Stockbroker's minimum commission at (say)	£25.00
Stamp Duty at 0.5%	£5.50
Contract levy (deals over £1,000)	£0.80
VAT at 15% on commission	£3.75

TOTAL A BUYER PAYS	£1,080.05

buying 2,500 shares in Bloggs and Bloggs plc

Consideration: 2,500 Bloggs and Bloggs plc at 418p		£10,450.00
Stockbroker's commission at (say) 1.65% on first £7,000	£115.50	
0.55% on balance of £3,450	£18.98	
[Total commission	£134.48]	
Stamp Duty at 0.5%		£52.50
Contract levy		£0.80
VAT at 15% on commission		£20.17

TOTAL A BUYER PAYS	£10,657.95

selling 250 shares in Bloggs and Bloggs plc

Consideration: 250 Bloggs and Bloggs at 410p[1]	£1,025.00
less Stockbroker's minimum commission at (say)	£25.00
Stamp Duty	-
Contract levy (deals over £1,000)	£0.80
VAT at 15% on commission	£3.75

TOTAL A SELLER GETS	£995.45

selling 2,500 shares in Bloggs and Bloggs plc

Consideration: 2,500 Bloggs and Bloggs at 410p[1]	£10,250.00
less Stockbroker's commission at (say) scale as above	£133.38
Stamp Duty	-
Contract levy	£0.80
VAT at 15% on commission	£20.00

TOTAL A SELLER GETS	£10,095.82

If you bought 250 Bloggs and Bloggs shares at 418p, the price would have to rise to about 454p – more than eight per cent up – before you could break even.

If you bought 2,500 Bloggs and Bloggs shares at 418p, the price would have to rise to about 443p – six per cent up – before you could break even.

[1] We have assumed a two per cent spread: i.e. bid price 410p when offer price 418p.

D-i-y share transfers

If you want to *give* the shares you own to someone else – husband or wife, say – you can normally do so without paying any Stamp Duty and without using (and having to pay for) the services of a stockbroker. This is how you go about it. Get a share transfer form (these are available from legal stationers). Fill it in and send it to the Office of the Controller of Stamps, Inland Revenue, West Block, Barrington Road, Worthing BN12 4SF. They will stamp it and return it to you. You should then send the transfer form and share certificate to the registrar of the company. They will alter their records and issue a share certificate in the name of the new owner.

The same d-i-y method – avoiding the services of a stockbroker – can also apply if you *sell* shares you own, though there may well be problems in deciding on what the price should be (which is, after all, what a stock market is for). In this case, however, Stamp Duty has to be paid – at the usual rate of 0.5 per cent, rounded up to the nearest 50p – and sent, with the share transfer form, to the Office of the Controller of Stamps.

For information on how to transfer the ownership of new issues, see page 46.

Buying new issues

All our earlier sections on how to deal in shares through a stockbroker or your bank might be new to you. And yet you may have a substantial shareholding in various companies already. No doubt it's because you bought by filling in an application form in one of the newspapers for one of the privatisation issues such as British Gas, Rolls-Royce, British Airways, or BAA – or having got the taste for share buying, have gone in for perhaps more adventurous non-privatisation new issues.

You might be planning to buy these new issues to hold them. Or you may be setting out to be a **stag**, and sell them straight away for a quick profit. The way you buy is quite different from buying already-existing shares. Here are the main do's and don'ts.

Types of new issues

Fixed-price offers for sale are the most common. The price is set beforehand, so you know exactly how much a share will cost. You might not have to pay the full price immediately, but pay in two or three instalments. Once you've bought the shares, it's important not to miss instalment payments. Always notify a change of address, so reminders can be sent to you. If you fail to pay by the due date, you can lose your shares.

Offers for sale by tender are more complicated. You have to write down on the application form the price you are prepared to pay for the shares, and the number you want. Then, when all the applications are in, a **striking price** is decided (based on numbers applied for and the sort of offers people have made). If your offer matches the striking price, or is above it, you get your shares at the striking price. If you've offered below the striking price, you won't get any shares at all.

However, *be warned*. A different method of tendering (and one that might be followed in later privatisations) was used with a quarter of the shares in the BAA launch. Here, a *cut-off price* was set. Applications *above* the cut-off price were met in full, *at whatever price was actually tendered.* Applications *at* the cut-off price got a proportion of the shares applied for; applications *below* the cut-off price got none. So it is important to read the terms of any tender offer with very great care – and to be wary of applying for more shares, or at a higher price, than you are prepared to pay for.

It's hard for novice investors to judge how much to tender: the best advice really is to watch for clues in the financial press for the sort of price that the large institutions will be pitching in at, and be cautious about offering more.

Applying for new issues

Application forms are included in the full prospectus for the sale, which may well appear in the newspapers, particularly the *Financial Times*. It's important to fill in the form carefully, following the instructions. These vary quite a lot, so don't assume the ordering or numbering of the form will be like any previous application you made. Pin your cheque to the form – paper clips can come adrift, and your cheque and form may get separated in a welter of applications.

Wrongly filled in forms, photocopies, and ones without their money may well be ruled invalid. Post your cheque and form in plenty of time to the correct address, or deliver it by hand. It must get there before the deadline.

New issues are often over-subscribed, and applications are scaled down, often in a way that favours the smaller investor. Or there may be a ballot, which might mean you'd get nothing at all. Your money, or the balance remaining after the scaled-down allocation, will be sent back to you.

There are no dealing costs when you apply for a new issue. You pay only the consideration (i.e. the actual cost of the shares). There's no VAT, no commission, no Contract levy and no Stamp Duty.

Multiple applications – filling in more than one form in your own name – may be outlawed in a new issue offer for sale. Check the prospectus very carefully to see whether this is the case. The penalties for breaking the rules and getting caught doing so are severe – and methods of detecting culprits are becoming increasingly sophisticated.

A **letter of allotment** (or letter of acceptance) is the next thing you will get if your application has been successful. If you acquire only a proportion of the shares you wanted, you'll get your money back at the same time. Then:

- If you want to keep your shares, do nothing, but put your letter of allotment away somewhere safe.
- If you want to sell all or part of your shares, find the **form of renunciation** (sometimes called form X) which is at the back of the allotment letter. You then proceed as if you're selling any other sort of shares, contacting your bank or stockbroker to deal for you, and sending the signed form of renunciation to them. You'll have to pay commission as usual, though some banks and brokers who've been involved in the new issue may offer cut-price dealing for a short period immediately after the issue. Dealings in new shares don't have to wait for settlement day to be paid up. They're cash deals – so you should get your money quickly. New issues continue to get this special treatment for four to six weeks after the issue. When you sell, you lose all the fringe benefits that come with the shares (e.g. vouchers for gas, etc.). And note: if you're buying new shares second-hand, you don't usually get these benefits passed on – and you'll have to pay up straight away, rather than wait for settlement day.
- If you want to get shares that have been bought in someone else's name on your behalf transferred to you, get them to fill in the form of renunciation to transfer the shares into your name. Send it back to the company, or the bank acting on its behalf, *not* to your bank or stockbroker.
- Don't try to deal in the shares before your letter of allotment arrives. You might have filled in the form or cheque wrongly, or it might never have arrived. Then you'll be left having to buy shares to meet your commitment, probably at a considerably higher price.

If payment is by instalments, your shares are called **partly paid**. The share price goes up by the amount of the instalment (or thereabouts) at about the time it falls due. If you sell the shares before an instalment is due, the buyer takes over the responsibility for the instalments.

Sometime after your shares have become fully paid, you will be sent the **share certificate**. Keep it in a safe place.

6 *Tax on shares*

There are three main types of tax you need to be aware of:

- Income tax on dividends.
- Capital gains tax on any capital gain you make.
- Inheritance tax if you leave shares as part of your estate when you die, or with some gifts during your lifetime.

Income tax

Dividends are liable to income tax with all the rest of your taxable income. But they are paid out to you with the equivalent of basic rate tax already deducted. Strictly speaking, this is because the company has already deducted advance corporation tax (ACT) from the dividend and paid it over to the taxman on your behalf. The company can later set the ACT it has already paid against its corporation tax bill for that accounting period. For the 1988–89 tax year, the rate of ACT is 25 per cent – the same as the basic rate of income tax.

Each dividend you get will be accompanied by a tax voucher (see page 48). This shows the dividend you are getting (after the deduction of tax) and the amount of your tax credit (the amount of tax that's been deducted). The dividend plus the tax credit equals the before-tax (gross) amount of the dividend: so if the dividend is £45 and the tax credit is £15, the gross amount is £45 + £15 = £60. To work out your tax bill you need to add this gross amount to the rest of your income.

Hang on to your tax vouchers: you should declare the amount of your dividends on your tax return, and the taxman may want to see the vouchers as proof that tax has been deducted.

All this means that:

- If you are a basic-rate taxpayer, you shouldn't have to worry about tax; the company's deduction has taken care of your liability. However, if you have a large amount of income from shares, or your income is near the limit for paying higher-rate tax, you will need to check that the gross amount of the dividends doesn't push you into the higher tax brackets. At present, any investment income a wife gets counts as her husband's income (though this will change in 1990).

0	British Components plc
1	Ordinary Shares of 25p each

BRITISH COMPONENTS

security code
012 – 90 – 68

Tax voucher

31st July, 1988

The attached warrant is in payment of the single dividend for the year ended 31st March, 1988, at the rate of 4.116p per share on the Ordinary Shares in respect of which you were the Registered Holder of Interim Rights on 11th June, 1988.

I certify that Advance Corporation Tax of an amount equal to that shown below as Tax Credit will be accounted for to the Collector of Taxes.

J. Smith Secretary

Silas Marner
Stone Cottage
Raveloe

Registrar:-
Lloyds Bank plc
Registrar's Department
Goring-by-Sea
Worthing, West Sussex
BN12 6DA

This voucher should be kept
It will be accepted by the
Inland Revenue as
evidence if you are entitled
to claim repayment of tax

holding	tax credit	dividend payable
reference 777/		
0050905	£2.06	***£8.23
200		

An example of a tax voucher.

- If you are a higher-rate taxpayer, you will have to pay higher-rate tax on the gross amount of your dividends – but the basic-rate tax counts as already paid. So if you are a 40 per cent taxpayer once the gross amount of the dividends is added to the rest of your income, you have to pay tax at $40 - 25 = 15$ per cent on the gross amount of your dividends. Any higher-rate tax due on dividends received in one tax year has to be paid on 1 December of the following tax year (or within 30 days of the date on the notice of assessment the taxman might send you, if later).
- If, once the gross dividend is added to the rest of your taxable income, you are a non-taxpayer, or should pay less tax than the amount deducted, you can claim tax back. You can either claim by filling in and sending back your tax return, if you get one, or by asking the taxman for form R40, if you don't.

Capital gains tax on the capital gain

You will have to worry about this tax only when you 'dispose' of things like shares, unit trusts, second homes, jewellery and antiques. Broadly speaking, a 'disposal' is any occasion on which you part with one of these things – e.g. by selling or giving them away. There's no capital gains tax on death, and there are a number of exemptions and reliefs which can cut down the tax – for example, only gains made after 31 March 1982 are now taxable. Most importantly, you pay no tax at all if the total gains from all your taxable disposals (after taking some reliefs into account) are below the annual capital gains tax threshold – £5,000 in the 1988–89 tax year.

Any gains above the capital gains tax threshold used to be taxed at a single rate of 30 per cent. But, from 6 April 1988, gains are taxed at the same rate of tax as you pay on your income: in the 1988–89 tax year, either 25 or 40 per cent.

Working out the capital gains tax on your shares can get very complicated if you buy shares in the same company at different times – see p52 for how this affects the tax. If you bought all your shares in one company at the same time, there are five steps to working out how much tax you are likely to have to pay:

Step 1
Take the amount you got from selling your shares, if you sold them, or their market value at the time if you gave them away.

Step 2
Deduct the expenses of buying and selling, e.g.:
- What you paid for the shares, if you bought them, or their market value

at the time if you were given or inherited them (this figure is called the 'initial value').
● Stockbroker's commission, Contract levy and Stamp Duty.

If you bought the shares before 31 March 1982 you generally use just the market value on that date unless the transitional rules described in 'Special cases' opposite apply.

If the answer you get from Steps 1 and 2, added to your gains after expenses from parting with other possessions, is below the capital gains tax threshold, there'll be no capital gains tax to pay. If it's above the tax threshold, there may be tax to pay. And if you end up with a minus figure from any of the disposals – i.e. you made a loss – make a note of it, because you can use it to reduce your taxable gains from other disposals, either in that tax year or in future years. Carry on to Step 3.

Step 3
Work out your *indexation allowance*. This stops you being taxed on gains you've made purely because of inflation since March 1982. To work it out you'll need to know the Retail Prices Index (RPI) for:

● The month in which you acquired the shares or incurred the expense, or March 1982 if later (RI).
● The month in which you parted with the shares (RD).

Then deduct RI from RD and divide the result by RI (work this out to three decimal places). You should end up with a figure that looks something like 0.223. Multiply each of your expenses (from Step 2) by that figure. (But if you acquired shares before 31 March 1982 see 'Special cases' opposite for the figure to multiply.) What you end up with is your indexation allowance.

For example, suppose you bought some shares for £2,000. The RPI when you bought them was 95, 115 when you sold them. Your indexation allowance is:

115 − 95 = 20
20 ÷ 95 = 0.211
0.211 × £2,000 = £422

Step 4
Deduct your indexation allowance from the figure you ended up with in Step 2 – even if that figure was a minus figure, you can use the allowance to increase your loss, or even to turn a gain into a loss.

Carrying on the example from Step 3, if you made a profit of £3,000 when you sold the shares (after deducting the purchase price and your expenses) the gain after indexation would be:

£3,000 − £422 = £2,578

If your profit had been, say, only £300 (not £3,000) you could still have deducted your indexation allowance: £422 deducted from £300 leaves *minus* £122, in other words a loss of £122 which you could set against other gains.

Step 5

Add up all your taxable gains from disposals during the tax year (after deducting indexation allowance). Deduct all your losses (after deducting indexation allowance). If the result is below the capital gains tax threshold (£5,000 in the 1988–89 tax year) there's no tax to pay. If it's over the threshold, look back to see if you made any losses in previous tax years, which you haven't already used to reduce tax bills. If you have, you can deduct those losses from your taxable gains after indexation.

You have to pay tax on anything over the capital gains tax threshold, at the same rate as you pay on your income – either 25 or 40 per cent in the 1988–89 tax year. If you pay income tax at the basic rate, but the amount of your taxable capital gains above the tax-free threshold *plus* your taxable income is more than the amount of the basic rate income tax band (£19,300 in 1988–89), you pay the higher rate on the excess. So if you had net taxable capital gains of £10,000 and taxable income of £10,500, say, you would pay capital gains tax at 25 per cent on the first £19,300, and at 40 per cent on the rest (£20,500 − £19,300 = £1,200).

There's space on your tax return to tell the taxman about any disposals over a certain value. If tax is due it has to be paid on 1 December after the end of the tax year in which the gains were made (i.e. 1 December 1989 for gains made in the 1988–89 tax year) or 30 days after the taxman issues his assessment, if later.

Special cases

● To work out the tax on shares owned before 31 March 1982, you generally use their market value on that date as their 'initial value'. However, if this would mean a bigger gain or loss than using their value when you actually acquired them (e.g. because their market value in 1982 was lower than what it cost you), *transitional rules* mean that you use the pre-1982 value. And, if the March 1982 value produces a gain where the pre-1982 value would have produced a loss (or vice versa), you are treated as if you had made neither a gain nor a loss. To keep things simple, you can elect always to use the March 1982 value, rather

Capital gains tax rules for shares bought in the same company at different times[1]

	Which shares?	How initial value (IV) is calculated	How indexation allowance is calculated
BATCH 1	Shares bought on same day	IV is purchase price (or market value) of shares bought on same day	No indexation allowance
BATCH 2	Shares bought in previous 10 days	IV is purchase price (or market value) of any shares bought in previous 10 days	No indexation allowance
BATCH 3	Shares acquired after 5 April 1982 and not in Batches 1 or 2	Shares are *pooled* – i.e. the IV of each share is the average cost of acquiring all the shares in the pool	The taxman first takes shares owned on 6 April 1985 and works out the allowance applying between date of acquisitions and 6 April 1985 for each separate lot of shares bought. Then each time shares are added to or withdrawn from the pool, the allowance is worked out again for the time between the last addition or withdrawal and date of disposal. On disposal, the allowance for each share is the average for all the shares in the pool
BATCH 4	Shares acquired after 5 April 1965 and before 6 April 1982	IV is the market value on 31 March 1982 *unless* using transitional rules (p51) when shares are pooled like Batch 3 shares, but in separate pool	Indexation allowance is worked out using either the actual cost or the market value on 31 March 1982, whichever figure is higher
BATCH 5	Shares acquired before 6 April 1965	IV is market value on 31 March 1982 unless using transitional rules, when shares are normally matched on a 'last in, first out' basis – i.e. IV is purchase price of last shares bought before 6 April 1965	Indexation allowance is worked out using either the actual cost or the market value on 31 March 1982, whichever figure is higher

---

[1] But disposed of after 6 April 1985 – there were different rules before then.

than the transitional rules: but once you have done this, you can't change your mind.

- For shares acquired before 31 March 1982, you either index-link the price you paid and other expenses to the RPI from March 1982 or you just index-link the shares at their market value on 31 March 1982 (and ignore pre-March 1982 expenses). The taxman uses whichever figure is highest, so that you get the most indexation allowance.
- If you're giving the shares away, you and the recipient can jointly apply for **hold-over relief**, which allows you to put off any tax until the recipient parts with the shares.
- Shares of the same type in the same company, acquired at different times, all look the same, and you can't tell which ones you've sold. So the taxman has special rules for deciding on their initial value. First the taxman divides the shares into a number of groups (or batches). Then he goes through the batches in order. The purchase price and indexation allowance are worked out according to the rules for the first batch in which you have shares. See the Table opposite for a summary of the rules, and the example below.

Example Horatio has bought shares in Victory Enterprises plc at different times over the years. He's now selling 5,000 of them. To work out his initial value and indexation allowance, the taxman first looks to see if Horatio bought any Victory shares on the same day as the sale (Batch 1) or the previous ten days (Batch 2). He didn't: but he did buy 3,000 shares in May 1985 (Batch 3). So the taxman uses the Batch 3 rules to work out the capital gains tax for 3,000 of the shares. Next the taxman goes on to see if Horatio has any Batch 4 shares. He has, so the taxman works out the tax on the remaining 2,000 shares being sold using the Batch 4 rules. He doesn't need to go back any further unless Horatio sells more of his shares.

Inheritance tax

When you die, your estate (or your beneficiaries under a will) may have to pay inheritance tax on any shares you leave or gave away during the previous seven years. There may also be tax to pay during your lifetime on any shares you give to some types of trust or to companies. *But*, whether on death or before, tax is due only if the total value of taxable gifts made in the previous seven years (plus the value of your estate on death) is over a certain limit (£110,000 in the 1988–89 tax year). There is no tax if the shares go to your husband or wife.

So most people need not worry about inheritance tax. For more details, look at Inland Revenue leaflet IHTI.

Tax tips

- Although capital gains and income are now taxed at the same rates, capital gains still have a tax advantage because the first slice of gains made in each tax year is tax-free. So you may be able to save tax by choosing shares that produce high capital growth rather than high income.
- There is no tax on shares held in Personal Equity Plans for the right length of time (see page 27). But the costs of investing in one are likely to outweigh the tax saving unless you are a higher-rate taxpayer or over the capital gains tax threshold, and willing to invest for some years.
- A higher-rate taxpayer and willing to take a risk? Consider investing in a Business Expansion Scheme (see page 115).
- If you are a non-taxpayer, or should pay less tax than has been deducted from your dividends, you can reclaim tax – but shares are probably not the most sensible investment for you anyway.
- Buying shares for children? Remember that if their income is below a certain limit (£2,605 in the 1988–89 tax year) they will be non-taxpayers and can reclaim any income tax deducted on share dividends. *Warning*: if you give money to your own children to invest, then any income from that investment will be taxed as yours, not your child's, unless it is below £5.
- Keep track of capital losses you make when you part with shares. You can use them to reduce your capital gains tax bill in future (unless they are losses made on a Personal Equity Plan).
- If you want to cash in some shares which will result in a capital gain above the annual tax-free limit, try to spread your sales over two or more tax years. That way you can make maximum use of your tax-free limit.
- But if your only reason for selling shares is to avoid tax, beware – any tax saving may be eaten up by the costs of buying and selling.

7 *If things go wrong*

There's no protection against losing money because you've chosen to invest in the wrong shares. But under the Financial Services Act – partly in force now, and substantially in force by the end of 1988 – there's some protection against rogues. 'Investment' is given a catch-almost-all description in the Act, and all businesses dealing in or advising on investments will have to be *authorised* as a condition of being allowed to carry on their business.

Under the Act, statutory powers to authorise and regulate investment businesses have been delegated to the new regulatory body, the Securities and Investments Board (SIB). SIB, in turn, has recognised five Self-Regulating Organisations (SROs) and nine professional bodies. The SRO for share-dealing businesses is The Securities Association (TSA), which has been set up by the Stock Exchange. Firms which advise on share-buying may be members of the Financial Intermediaries, Managers and Brokers Regulatory Organisation (FIMBRA). Not all the regulatory powers in the Act have been transferred to SIB, however. In particular, SIB is not concerned with investigations into **insider dealing**, which remain a matter for the Department of Trade and Industry, nor for the policing of takeovers and mergers (the responsibility of the Panel on Takeovers and Mergers).

Investment businesses can choose whether to be authorised directly by SIB, or by being members of an appropriate SRO, or by being a member of a recognised professional body (e.g. solicitors, accountants). It will be a criminal offence for an investment business to operate without being authorised – though at the time of writing (May 1988) many firms have only *interim authorisation*, which allows them to continue in business until they have been vetted. The legislation provides SIB with a variety of sanctions against erring investment businesses. These range from rather feeble (private) reprimands, through public reprimands, taking action in the courts to obtain restitution of investors' money, suspension, and, in the last resort, withdrawal of authorisation (which would ban the firm from doing business altogether). SIB also has powers over erring SROs – which it could, in the last resort, de-recognise.

The Act sets out the guiding principles for the conduct of business rules which investment businesses must follow, and SIB was given the task of translating these principles into detailed rules. Each SRO has then had to draw up its own rules – which are required to be 'equivalent' to SIB's. The SRO – or SIB, for businesses which are directly authorised by SIB – then has to ensure that the rules are being observed, and has powers to impose disciplinary measures if they are not. SIB, in turn, has the task of ensuring that the SROs are kept up to the mark.

Here is an outline of what the rules require:

- Those carrying out investment business must be 'fit and proper' to do so.
- Investment businesses have to have regard for the investor's best interests when giving any advice, and therefore have to do their best to be aware of the investor's circumstances. There normally have to be written customer agreements with investors in shares (other than dealing-only investors). These include details of the services being provided and their cost, set out investment objectives, and warn on the risks of certain types of investments.
- For most transactions, the rule of best execution applies – which means that the firm must carry out a deal on the best terms available. And in such cases the firm has a duty to disclose material information (that, for example, the firm is itself a market-maker in the shares concerned).
- A number of the investor protection rules do not apply to professional or business investors, nor to people who are classed as experienced investors in their customer agreements. So take extra care if this applies to you.
- Unsolicited visits and telephone calls to sell shares are – as in the past – banned (though not calls to sell unit trusts or life insurance).
- All published recommendations, including those in share tipsheets, must be properly researched. This does not mean, of course, that the recommendations are in any way guaranteed to produce results – but at least they should not be made recklessly or fraudulently.
- Investment businesses must make proper arrangements for the segregation of clients' money (e.g. money awaiting investment) to reduce the scope for fraud and for any losses to investors if the investment business should fail. But it will be October 1988 at the earliest before this rule comes fully into force.
- There must be arrangements for the investigation of investors' complaints by the SRO or SIB – in some cases including, at the end of the line, independent investigation. Before you have dealings with an investment business, it will be worth checking on which is the relevant SRO, or whether the business has been authorised directly by SIB – so that you know who to direct complaints to if you cannot get a satisfactory answer from the business itself.

● From the end of August 1988, there must be compensation for investors if an authorised investment business fails, up to a limit of £48,000 (full protection for the first £30,000 of your investment then protection for 90 per cent of the next £20,000). Some SROs may decide to pay more than this. A limit of £48,000 is in some cases worse – though in others much better – than what used to apply before this part of the Act came into force. For instance, if a stockbroker fails there is at present (May 1988) a compensation fund from which payments of up to £250,000 can be made (more in certain circumstances); with other share dealers there is currently no compensation fund.

But it is of course one thing to have a set of rules, another to have those rules rigorously enforced. Much depends on the amount of zeal with which SIB and the SROs carry out their monitoring and enforcement, and on how the SROs – which are, after all, *self*-regulators, whose governing boards are dominated by members of the industry involved – perceive their responsibilities to investors.

So it is only after the Act has been in force for some time that it will be possible to judge how effective it is in protecting investors. Nor do we yet know what it will all cost. It is of course investors who will be footing the bill – in part visibly (e.g. the Contract levy when buying or selling shares) but for the most part invisibly (included in commission and charges). Whatever the outcome, however, investors can never afford to sit back and assume that the Financial Services Act will look after all their interests. Here are some of the things that investors should continue to be watchful about:

● Despite the protection given by the rules, the interests of the private investor may not always come first. Most stockbrokers are now owned by financial conglomerates, which include banks and merchant banks, with possibly very different interests from those of investors. Stockbrokers also act for companies whose shares are traded on the Stock Exchange.

● Some stockbrokers now act as market-makers – which means that they trade in shares on their own account. There are rules and **Chinese walls** to ensure that this does not influence their recommendations, but it is too early to say how effective the rules (or their enforcement) will be.

● In the past it has not been entirely unknown for share tipsters in newspapers and magazines to recommend shares which they already own. The Financial Services legislation sets standards for share tipsheets.

● Remember that brokers hope to earn commission from you – so do not be tempted to over-trade (buy and sell excessively). And if professionals are managing your share investments for you, watch out for **churning** (excessive buying and selling, mainly to earn commission).

- And finally, remember that the legislation is not there to take the risk out of investment, nor is it there to protect you from your own foolishness. Its stated aim is, primarily, to ensure that there are properly run markets in which investors and investment businesses will have confidence.

Section II

Choosing shares

8 *The risks involved*

As an investor – or potential investor – you'll be told time and again (not least, in this book) that shares are a risky investment. What sorts of risk do you face? And what steps can you take to make sure that you don't take on greater risks than you'd be comfortable with?

The risks you face

Company risk

The result of investing in a particular company will depend – at least in part – on how well that company competes in the market-place. The company's profits (and its share price) will depend on such factors as how well it's managed, whether demand is maintained for its products, and how innovative it is when faced with changes in the market-place. At the extreme, you face the risk that the company is unable to compete at all, goes into decline and finally goes bust. You may find that you've lost all your money, since the liquidator will pay the taxman, employees, creditors and loan stock holders what's owed them before distributing anything to shareholders.

Market risk

However well run and competitive a particular company is, its share price will be affected by movements in the stock market as a whole. These movements, in turn, depend on the prevailing mood among investors. If they're optimistic about future prospects, share prices in general rise; if they take a gloomy view of the future, share prices tend to fall. The mood among investors is influenced by general economic prospects, government actions, international events, foreign stock markets (most stock markets tend more and more to move together) and so on. But at times, there appears to be no rational explanation for swings up (or down).

When share prices are in general rising, this is known as a **bull market**; when they tend to be falling, this is known as a **bear market**. From early 1975 until October 1987, share prices tended to move upwards (a bull market) with occasional hiccups on the way. But the trouble with a 12-year period of upward growth was that some investors started thinking that a period when share prices slid downward (a bear market) was a thing of the past. And many of the newer and younger professional advisers have had little or no experience of handling a bear market of any length.

So Black Monday (19 October 1987) was a day that investors – and their advisers – are not quickly going to forget. That was the day that the US stock market crashed, swiftly followed by the steepest-ever one-day fall on the London stock market, and falls on other stock markets around the world. On 20 October, newspaper headlines announced 'City sees £50 billion wiped off stock values'. On average, share prices on the London stock market fell by around 10 per cent on 19 October, and recorded a fall of around 30 per cent during the last two weeks in October. After the event, experts offered confident explanations of why the crash happened – though one wonders why they didn't reveal beforehand that the crash was about to happen.

It is a feature of a bear market that the majority of share prices fall. The risk of the share price being dragged down in this way – irrespective of the merits of the company – is **market risk**.

At the time of writing (May 1988) no one can of course say whether the October 1987 crash was the start of a prolonged bear market, or simply a very nasty hiccup with recovery around the corner. It may be worth noting, however, that the bear market of 1973 and 1974 was very much more severe. Over that period, shares on average lost rather more than half their value (or three-quarters if inflation is taken into account). It was not until 1977 that average share prices recovered to the monetary level of their peak in 1972 (and, of course, by then inflation had eroded their value). Market risk, even after the fall of October 1987, remains a major peril.

Building up your portfolio

There are only three fundamental principles on which all your investment decisions should be based:

1 You are unlikely to have supernormal investment powers, so you would be wise to assume that you will not be able, consistently, to pick shares that will outperform the market average; *and* that you will not be able, consistently, to take the right decisions on the timing of when to buy and sell (see Chapter 10). All your investment decisions ought to be made in the light of these uncomfortable truths.
2 You should try to keep your exposure to market risk and company risk at a level which is acceptable to you.
3 You should keep all unnecessary expenses to a minimum – such as buying and selling expenses (e.g. stockbrokers' commission).

By applying these three principles, you will be led to the following set of investment strategies when choosing your portfolio of shares:

Keeping the risk down

If you've decided to keep your risk to a minimum, one of the first steps you could take is to avoid direct investment in shares altogether. You could, instead, take the indirect route via unit trusts, say (see Chapter 2), or you could decide to cut down on the amount you had earmarked for direct investment in shares. If you'd initially decided on putting £20,000 into shares, cutting it to £10,000 (and putting the other £10,000 into an investment where the value doesn't fluctuate) means that only half your money is exposed to these risks. But, of course, you've also cut down your chances of making substantial gains.

Once you've come to a final decision on how much money you're prepared to put at risk, adopt the following risk-reduction strategy.

Don't invest in just one company

Doing so exposes you not just to market risk, but also to the full force of company risk. Of course, you could do very well, but you run the risk of doing extremely badly indeed. *Which?* has done some research into what might happen if you bought only one share; we found that, four years after making a notional investment of £1,000, you could be left with anything from nothing to £10,000. If you had spread your money over more companies, your chances of an extreme result became much smaller. As the number of shares you invest in increases, you start exposing yourself to a rather different problem – i.e. a reducing chance of outperforming the market. By the time you reach 16 shares or more, the chances of all of them doing much worse than average are remote. Unfortunately the chances of a much above-average return are also extremely small. And having *too* many shares faces you with other problems – more administration to keep track of them, and increased dealing costs (depending on how much you have to invest).

So how many companies' shares should you invest in? To achieve a worthwhile reduction in risk, you should certainly go for four or five companies; you could consider investing in up to ten. Beyond that you get into the area of diminishing returns – not much more in the way of risk reduction, and an increasingly remote chance of beating the market average (if that is your aim).

Don't go for just one industry

It would be prudent to choose the shares of companies in different industries, because there is also the risk that a whole industry – and the shares of most of the companies in it – may hit the doldrums for a while. ('Industries', in this context, includes services such as banking, insurance, tourism, etc.) Opposite, you'll see a section of the *Financial Times*-Actuaries indexes which measure the performance of particular industries (as well as giving an indication of average share performance through the All-Share Index at the bottom of the Chart). From even just this one example, you can see that different industries perform very differently over a particular period (and also that their past performance is not a guide to their future performance).

When selecting your different industries, you should choose ones whose areas of work are as independent of one another as possible, so that hard times for one company would not automatically mean hard times for any of the others. This may not always be a very simple task: a company may have a range of interests, or interests that you might not suspect from the company's name – so some enquiries into what work a company is actually doing may be necessary (see Chapter 12).

Choose your companies with risk in mind

As explained on page 37, quoted shares are divided into four categories – alpha, beta, gamma and delta – according to how large the company is and how actively the shares are traded. The alpha stocks cover the 100 or so largest and most actively traded shares. To keep your risk to a minimum, concentrate on these large and well-established companies (though remember that no share is risk-free). An advantage of alpha stocks is that you're unlikely to find it hard to sell shares in such companies should you wish to – there's always a ready market for them. In addition, there's sufficient competition between the market-makers dealing in these shares to make sure that the spread between **bid** and **offer price** is a narrow one.

FT-ACTUARIES INDICES

**These Indices are the joint compilation of the Financial Times,
the Institute of Actuaries and the Faculty of Actuaries**

EQUITY GROUPS & SUB-SECTIONS	Thursday July 9 1987						Wed July 8	Tues July 7	Mon July 6	Year ago (approx.)
Figures in parentheses show number of stocks per section	Index No.	Day's Change %	Est. Earnings Yield % (Max.)	Gross Div. Yield % (ACT at 27%)	Est. P/E Ratio (Net)	xd adj. 1987 to date	Index No.	Index No.	Index No.	Index No.
1 CAPITAL GOODS (212)	1000.90	+0.6	6.85	2.72	18.29	10.75	994.72	992.12	984.77	735.13
2 Building Materials (29)	1324.32	+0.4	6.55	2.59	19.12	13.90	1319.45	1295.24	1288.96	824.59
3 Contracting, Construction (33)	1852.54	+0.6	6.47	2.58	20.74	19.38	1842.06	1826.46	1807.82	1267.44
4 Electricals (13)	2670.24	+1.3	5.68	2.98	22.63	36.50	2637.80	2580.86	2573.29	1891.41
5 Electronics (35)	2143.26	+0.5	7.07	2.29	18.10	15.24	2131.81	2152.72	2130.92	1657.88
6 Mechanical Engineering (60)	529.39	+0.8	7.62	3.19	16.47	7.68	525.28	527.98	524.82	418.47
8 Metals and Metal Forming (7)	567.29	+0.9	6.91	2.77	17.65	6.88	562.47	565.21	565.90	386.40
9 Motors (14)	382.30	+1.0	7.99	2.77	14.55	3.42	378.62	377.83	377.66	312.99
10 Other Industrial Materials (21)	1641.03	+0.6	6.02	2.97	20.03	20.86	1631.20	1625.63	1618.65	1319.42
21 CONSUMER GROUP (185)	1362.01	+0.2	5.80	2.48	22.12	13.72	1358.94	1364.32	1357.43	931.95
22 Brewers and Distillers (22)	1245.50	+1.1	7.53	2.86	16.71	11.67	1231.37	1252.14	1245.82	951.97
25 Food Manuf.	1049.01	−0.2	6.70	2.91	19.37	14.27	1050.99	1060.87	1050.29	607.66
26	2560.33	+0.3	5.01	2.25	27.20			74.90	2593.10	1840.30
	82.75	−0.4	3.91	1.69					2529.84	1571.23
(1)		+1.2	5.70							
...(0)	1313....									
Financial (28)	570.27	+1....				5.89	562.59	556..		
Investment Trusts (91)	1126.14	+1.1	—	2.13	—	10.97	1113.49	1111.12	111...	
... Mining Finance (2)	583.91	+4.5	5.80	2.85	19.81	6.79	559.01	546.51	534.11	267....
91 Overseas Traders (10)	1150.70	+0.5	7.87	4.09	15.08	23.27	1145.18	1137.51	1128.60	685.49
99 ALL-SHARE INDEX(721)	1199.06	+0.7	—	2.94	—	13.85	1191.17	1193.44	1187.67	805.63
	Index	Day's	Day's	Day's	July	July h	July 3	July 2	Year ago	

These *Financial Times*-Actuaries indexes all started at 100 in April 1962. By around 9 July *1986* (see last column on the right), the shares of companies in the electronics category had averaged a rise to 1657.88. By contrast, the index for shares of building material companies had risen to 824.59 – only around half as much. However, if you look at the first column of figures – the index at 9 July 1987 – and get out a calculator, you will find that electronics shares averaged an increase of 29 per cent over the previous 12 months, compared with a 60 per cent rise by building materials firms (shares as a whole went up 49 per cent).

On most days you'll find a list of alpha stocks in the *Financial Times*, *The Independent* and *The Times* (and the share prices in the *Financial Times* also show which are alpha stocks).

Advice from a broker may help you in your search for low-risk shares. You could suggest to your broker that you're looking for defensive shares with a **beta** of less than 1 (see page 77 of Chapter 10 to bring yourself up to date on betas). Don't be surprised if your stockbroker raises an eyebrow – it's rare for such a proposal to be put by a private investor. But if you persist, your stockbroker can certainly track down this information on particular shares. As always, there's a trade-off between cutting down risk and at the same time cutting down your chances of outperforming the market. By going for shares with low betas, you'll be going for shares that are likely to fluctuate less than the market as a whole – down *or* up.

If your aim is risk reduction, there are certain shares you should definitely avoid, notably:

- those sold on the Unlisted Securities Market (USM)
- those sold on the Over-The-Counter (OTC) Market, or the Stock Exchange's Third Market
- those in Business Expansion Scheme (BES) companies.

In Chapter 18 we give more details about these markets. But basically you'd be buying into a relatively small company, often one with a short trading history. You'll find it easy enough to buy shares – but when you come to sell, you may hit one of their biggest snags. You may find that no one is making a market in them, and it's extremely difficult to get rid of them except at a rock-bottom price.

Invest in some foreign companies
Spreading your investments around different countries is another way of cutting down your risk – it will mean that the outcome of your investment won't depend entirely on the UK stock market. By choosing investments in a cross-section of countries, you reduce your risk of them all doing badly at once. You can get an indication of this effect by looking at the performance of unit trusts. The top and bottom performers in any year are often those specialising in a particular country. And from one year to the next you'll find that the best (and worst) specialisations change – so in one year you'll find European trusts best and Australian worst, and in another year quite the opposite may apply.

Investing directly in foreign shares can be done through a stockbroker – but you're likely to find it expensive and it can lead to administrative problems (with, for example, dividends, tax, etc.). The most convenient way for most investors to 'go foreign' is likely to be by investing in unit trusts or investment trust companies specialising in foreign companies. Chapter 18 gives more details.

If you're prepared to live dangerously
If you've got money to spare – i.e. money you could afford to lose – you may decide to accept a high level of risk in the hope of making a killing. If this is the case, you simply do the opposite of the risk-reduction advice given above. So you back what you reckon is a red-hot tip and go for shares in just one company. You may even be tempted by shares sold on

the Unlisted Securities Market, or a Business Expansion Scheme venture. Or you may decide to invest in a foreign company (and nothing else) rather than going for a spread of countries including the UK. Take this approach only if you're prepared to look on your investment in shares as an out-and-out gamble.

So which shares should you buy?

Sadly, neither this book, nor your professional adviser, nor your friend in the pub is going to give you an answer to that question to guarantee your fortunes. As described in Chapter 10, the current market price of a share is not a value plucked out of the air. It's likely to take into account all the information publicly known about the company – and after hundreds of professional analysts have searched and scanned through the data. Don't be tempted by a 'cheap' share – there are likely to be good reasons for its low price.

The guidelines above will help to narrow down your choice. You'll also need to take into account what you're hoping to get out of your investment – income or capital growth (see below). Your next step is to glean information from the financial press, from your advisers and friends, and from your own knowledge of particular companies or industries. But, at the end of the day, you'll have to take the plunge – either by following your own hunch or somebody else's.

Do you want income or capital growth?

The return from shares can come in the form of income (through dividends) or through capital growth in the value of the shares – or, you hope, through both. If your major objective is to get a high income from your investment, shares with a reasonably high **dividend yield** are ones to consider. The dividend yield tells you the income you'd get from each £100 you invested in those shares. There is normally little relationship between the yield of a share and its riskiness (though if the dividend yield is exceptionally high, this implies that the share price is depressed – which may or may not be for good reasons).

If, on the other hand, you are looking for growth in the value of your investment, and do not need a high starting income, you should look at shares with the best prospects of overall growth – taking account of hoped-for capital gains, and of dividends. Remember that the taxman still treats capital gains more favourably than dividends – by giving you an annual tax-free allowance on capital gains (see page 49). So it can still make sense for a taxpayer (and particularly a higher rate taxpayer) to give rather more weight to prospects of capital gain, than of current income.

Attracted by new issues?

Government privatisations – involving new issues of millions of shares and what seemed to be a guaranteed quick buck for anyone lucky enough to be allocated any – may shake your trust in all the warnings given so far. And some new issues of private companies may have seemed to reinforce that message. However, don't assume that what applies to buying new issues always goes for buying shares more generally.

With a new issue, you usually pay a set price, and *not* the market price. The set price is often pitched at a lower level to try to make sure that all the shares are taken up (and with some privatisations, to widen share-ownership). This means that when the shares do start to be traded, there's often short-term money to be made. But bear in mind that with popular issues you may end up allocated only a small number of shares, and your gain would be severely dented by selling costs. For example, with the BAA privatisation, investors going for the fixed-price shares were allocated only 100 shares each. They could have made around £45 by selling straight away, but around half of that would have gone in selling costs. And don't forget that privatisation may still be vulnerable to political pressure.

Even with new issues, you're not guaranteed a profit – the set price could fail to find favour with investors and you'd then have bought at a high price. Or you could find that the market as a whole had slumped before you'd had time to sell your shares. Nor is the buying of new issues a good way to build up a portfolio: you're likely to end up with most shares in the unpopular issues, fewest in the popular ones.

When to buy and sell

As with which shares to buy in the first place, there's no magic answer to when to part with your money and when to cash in your investment. And these decisions can make a crucial difference to the outcome of your investment – indeed, they may matter more than *which* shares you've chosen.

Be wary of patent methods of picking the 'best' times to buy and sell. If such methods worked, you'd find that investments such as unit trusts managed by professionals (who could buy in whatever skills were needed) would outperform the market as a whole. As you'll see from Chapter 10, this is not the case. And though it's possible with the benefit of hindsight to spot the times when you ought to have bought (or sold) particular shares, what's not possible is to change that hindsight into a crystal ball for the future. You'll find that as shares approach a new high, there will be lots of optimists (professional and private investors alike) who reckon prices will go yet higher. And the reverse applies when prices go down.

Though it's impossible to gauge the right time to buy or sell, you can adopt an approach to cut your risks (though also your chances of making bumper gains). So, for example, if prices look low when you want to sell, you could decide to sell only part of your share holding and review the situation later. Similarly, if prices look high when you want to invest, you could hold some of your money in reserve in the hope of getting a better price later.

If all this sounds gloomy, once you've built up your portfolio you could consider adopting the approach outlined below.

Buy and hold

It's tempting to think that you can buy and sell shares and keep picking the ones that will be winners (and the right time to get in and out of them). As we've explained above, this is a delusion. So a policy of buy and hold would be a sensible one to follow. This means that once you've built up a portfolio, you resist the temptation to keep switching it around. In the long run this is likely to give you better results – not least because you save on buying and selling costs. You also postpone any capital gains tax bill. The costs of buying and selling are not trivial – as we've shown on page 43, they are likely to amount to around six to eight per cent of the money invested. And if you get caught for capital gains tax, the costs would be even higher. It may be suggested to you that, each year, you should sell enough shares to use up your tax-free capital gains allowance. Be wary of this advice – what you save on capital gains tax may well be more than cancelled out by the costs involved.

Do not necessarily think that you should tidy up your portfolio by selling off small shareholdings, or be tempted to 'take profits' on small amounts of shares when the price of your shares has risen. These operations, too, will cost you money.

9 *Types of shares*

Finding your way around the stock market is daunting for the novice investor. It makes life easier if you know some of the different ways in which shares are categorised.

Sectors

The 2,600 UK companies traded on the Stock Exchange are divided into groups, according to what the companies do. There are a number of broad headings like Capital Goods, Consumer Goods (durable) and Consumer Goods (non-durable) which are divided into a number of smaller groups, known as sectors. Companies in each sector are involved in similar types of business. For example, the Consumer Goods (non-durable) group is divided into 20 sectors including breweries, hotels and caterers, milling and flour, newspapers and periodicals, leather, and toys and games.

Newspapers that publish a daily shares listing usually use some variation of the Stock Exchange system. However, they can't be as detailed as the full Stock Exchange classification. Companies have to pay to have details of their shares included in newspaper listings, so information on some shares (generally only the most obscure) is missing. And, although newspapers generally use the Stock Exchange classification, they amalgamate some sectors into one. Take the *Financial Times*, for example, which publishes the most comprehensive list of shares. Where the Stock Exchange has different sectors for department stores, furnishing stores, mail-order stores, multiple stores, clothing, cotton and synthetic, wool and miscellaneous textiles, the *Financial Times* has only one, Drapery and stores. So if you want to see the full list, you'll need to consult the Stock Exchange Daily Official List (try your local library).

The *Financial Times* also contains the FT-Actuaries indexes (see page 63). These are weighted indexes, published every day, which show how individual sectors are performing. The index of each sector is based on the performance of a number of shares in that sector, giving more weight to the more important shares.

Fund managers of the big institutions, like pension funds and insurance companies, may invest in hundreds of shares across most, or even all, sectors. So a fund manager will find the FT-Actuaries indexes particularly useful. To begin with, the fund manager is likely to plan his investment strategy by sector. Later, if he believes that breweries, say, are likely to do well, he will invest more heavily in that sector. Having made decisions about sectors, he will then decide which shares to go for.

Fund managers can go about building a portfolio in this way because they are able to invest in a broad range of shares in each sector they choose. Few private investors will be able to do this, since they will be limited to one or two shares in any one sector. It's important to remember that the sector index gives only an overall picture – even in a successful sector, some shares may do badly. So for the private investor, the choice of share is as important as the choice of sector.

Despite this, the sector classifications are useful for judging how your shares are faring. There's no point in comparing a brewery share with a share in an oil company. Grouping similar companies together lets you run your eyes down the list and see which companies are doing better or worse than the norm. (See Chapter 11 for how to use newspapers to help you compare companies.)

But it pays to be slightly cautious when you're using the sector classification. The whole point of judging shares against those in similar industries is that they are all subject to some general conditions – if brewing is in a slump, all breweries should suffer more or less equally. So any deviation from the norm must be due to something unique to that company. This is fine as a theory, but some of the sectors – particularly in newspapers – are quite broad, and group together companies that are likely to be subject to quite different economic conditions. The leisure sector in the *Financial Times*, for example, includes London Weekend Television, Saga Holidays, the Virgin Group and Tottenham Hotspur Football Club. And some companies do a range of different things, so their inclusion in a particular sector may be misleading. You may need to do a bit of homework to ensure that you're really comparing like with like.

Alpha, beta, gamma, delta

When the Stock Exchange introduced SEAQ, the computerised share price information system, it initiated a new system of share classification.

Shares are classified as alphas, betas, gammas or deltas depending on how large the company is and how actively its shares are traded. There are currently around 100 alpha stocks, 600 betas, and 1,700 gammas with the rest being deltas, but the numbers aren't fixed. As a company grows, or its shares are traded more actively, it can move up a section, so the number of shares in each section frequently changes.

Most alpha stocks are household names: Barclays, Boots, British

Telecom, Hanson Trust, Rolls-Royce and Unilever, to take a few at random. They are the very biggest and most popular companies on the Stock Exchange.

On SEAQ, there will usually be at least ten market-makers in each alpha stock, and all deals will rapidly appear on SEAQ screens. In addition, some newspapers publish daily lists of the deals done in alpha stocks, so you can easily see which ones are being heavily traded. Although in number alpha stocks make up less than five per cent of companies quoted on the Stock Exchange, they account for some two-thirds of the volume of Stock Exchange business.

A beta stock will have at least five market-makers. Prices of alpha and beta stocks are 'firm'. This means that the market-maker will buy and sell at the prices quoted on SEAQ – so long as a marketable quantity of shares is involved (usually 1,000, but sometimes fewer).

Prices of gamma stocks quoted on SEAQ are indications only. Deals in gamma stocks are not reported until the following day.

Delta stocks – the remaining UK companies on the Stock Exchange – do not appear on SEAQ. A broker will use the TOPIC system (see page 37) for a guide to prices.

Blue chips

Blue chips (originally a term used in gambling) are shares in the largest companies quoted on the Stock Exchange. There's no definitive list of blue chip shares, but it's generally said to include all companies with a market capitalisation (number of shares multiplied by share price) of more than £500m. It's fairly safe to assume that all alpha stocks are included.

You may hear it said that blue chips are the safest shares. This is true as far as it goes. Because of their size blue chip companies are most unlikely to go bust overnight, or to drop dramatically in price (although this can happen). But there's no guarantee that investors will show a profit. Just like any other share, blue chips can go down in value.

The affairs of blue chip companies are well reported. We've already seen that deals in alpha stocks are published daily in some newspapers. In addition to this, blue chips feature fairly regularly in the City pages – and sometimes the news pages – of many newspapers. This makes it easy for someone with shares in a blue chip company to keep track of his or her investment.

So should the private investor stick with blue chips? It largely depends on how much risk you're prepared to accept (we go into this in more detail in Chapter 8). But, for most people, it makes sense to keep a fairly substantial part of your portfolio in relatively safe shares, like blue chips.

Growth stocks

Certain shares are sometimes temptingly described as **growth stocks**. Growth stocks are those shares that seem to do consistently better than the market as a whole. A typical growth stock is a fairly young company in a burgeoning sector of the economy. It will plough its profits back into the business to promote expansion. Each injection of capital generates more growth, which, in turn, generates more profits. If this is successful, it can go on for many years. A company that wants to grow still more rapidly may attempt to do so by taking over other companies. Some companies have succeeded as growth stocks almost entirely on the strength of takeovers. The Hanson Trust is perhaps the best-known example.

A company that is putting its profits back into the business may have little money to pay out as a dividend – or, in some cases, nothing at all. Because the share price is high, one of the tell-tale signs of a growth stock is a high **price/earnings ratio** (PE). The PE of a growth stock may easily be two or three times the PE for other companies in the same sector. The high PE ratio demonstrates that the market is expressing confidence in the company. It is prepared to accept little or no dividends at the moment, because it expects great things of the company.

The market is strict about what it classes as a growth stock. Some companies grow in cycles. A period of rapid expansion is followed by a trough; then comes another period of growth, then a further trough. The market may be prepared to put up with one or two small troughs. But if it happens too often, investors' confidence – essential to the continued success of a growth stock – will be lost.

Growth stocks are usually found in high-flying industries, particularly during a bull market. Over the last few years, several growth stocks have cropped up in high technology (computers, etc.), advertising and retailing. They quite often turn up on the USM, perhaps based on a single innovation or on the talents of a few people.

Growth stocks are wonderful so long as they're growing. But if the market loses confidence – perhaps because the person who built up the company leaves or because its formerly innovative product has been overtaken by something new – the share price can take a tumble.

The graph on page 72 charts the progress of Next, a typical growth share. As Hepworths, an unexciting menswear retailer, the company performed competently but unspectacularly for a number of years. In 1982 it opened the chain of Next shops, selling moderately priced, fashionable women's clothing. The idea was an immediate success and the company's shares took off. Hepworths changed their name to Next in 1986 and

Graph showing the progress of Next.

opened a chain of men's shops, followed by shops selling furniture and accessories. The price of Next shares rose dramatically from 1982 to 1987. In common with most other companies, they suffered in the stock market crash of October 1987. However, their share price in early 1988 was still more than five times higher than in 1982. Of course, there's no guarantee that it will remain high.

Buying shares for income

If you particularly want an income, you might first consider putting some or all of your money in other types of investment like government stocks or some unit trusts (see Chapter 2).

However, there are shares that will give you a higher than normal yield. This may be because although the share price has fallen recently, the directors are keeping the dividend at its previous level. They may be doing this because they believe that the company's problems are temporary and the share price will recover (for this reason, shares in this situation are sometimes called 'recovery stocks'). Or they may be keeping the dividend high so as not to destroy investors' confidence in the company.

If the business does recover, investors will do well, but there are two things to bear in mind. The dividend may be high at the moment, but the company could cut it if things don't improve. And the market may be avoiding the shares for very good reasons. If the company doesn't extricate itself from its difficulties and the share price doesn't improve, those who invested for income will be left to rue their decision.

10 *Share analysis*

The Eldorado that every investor seeks is a system of share analysis which will enable him to make an infallible choice of stock market winners. There is no shortage of systems. But despite the confident recommendations of stockbrokers, and despite the successes claimed by the experts – from professional fund managers to share tipsters – there is absolutely no proof that any of the methods of share analysis gives a reliable or usable method of picking out winning shares. On the contrary, extensive research suggests that it is impossible to devise a system that would be effective in identifying the shares which are likely to be winners, or the 'right' times to buy and sell.

Much of this research originated in universities and business schools in the United States in the 1960s, but has since been taken up by academics in other countries as well. A great deal of the research has been concerned with the **Efficient Market Hypothesis**. The gist of this theory is that share prices fully reflect all available information about a company. Research into this has shown pretty conclusively that share prices reflect all past information about price movements, earnings, and so on. In other words, any studies of the past performance can't give a guide to the future. There is also strong evidence that share prices reflect all publicly available information, such as announcements of results, rights issues, and so on. Ideally, an efficient market has the following characteristics: dealing costs are sufficiently low that they do not interfere with investors' intentions to buy or sell, all information is freely and widely available, investors draw the same conclusions from the available information. In practice, even if these conditions are not fully met, it seems that most share markets closely approximate efficient behaviour.

The inescapable conclusion of all this research is that a company's shares must at any time be 'correctly' priced – it is impossible for them to be 'cheap' or 'dear' as against some underlying valuation, because the price already reflects all available information, including any 'underlying valuations'. The only reason for the share price to change is if some previously unknown information becomes available. Since that information was previously unknown, it couldn't have been predicted. Thus, it would have been impossible to forecast the share price movement in advance.

Despite the strength of the Efficient Market Hypothesis and the very good evidence to support it, enormous sums are spent by fund managers, investment analysts and other experts whose task is to identify the shares and sectors which will outperform the rest of the market, and to forecast the best times to buy into or sell out of these shares and sectors. And it's not just the professionals who remain firmly convinced that it is possible to forecast investment returns in this way. The demand from private investors supports a huge industry of investment advisers and share tipsters who are looked on to provide thoroughly researched and learned opinions on the shares and times to buy and sell.

So are all these experts wasting their time? Well, yes and no. The research is strongly against their being able to select winning shares. But the activities of these experts are important to the creation and mainten-ance of an efficient market. Their dedication to seeking out and analysing information, and to acting on or publishing their findings, helps to ensure not only that information is available but also that the majority of investors have ready access to it. The paradox is that the more successful the experts are in creating the conditions for an efficient market, the more unlikely it is that any scope remains for them to find and take advantage of 'incorrectly' priced shares.

This does not mean that the investor should totally dismiss the various other schools of share analysis. There are sufficient devotees of some of these schools that their collective actions can themselves cause a movement in share prices – at least in the short term. So it is useful for even a small investor to have a basic understanding of how the other investors in the market are operating.

Methods of share analysis

Fundamental analysis

Analysts of this school of thought start with the view that, over a long period of time, the price of a company's shares will tend to match the underlying value of the company. This generally won't simply be the value of assets published in a company's report and accounts. The value tries to take account of the ability of those assets to generate profits in the future. So, for example, an analyst looking at an oil company's stake in a North Sea field is unlikely to take the value of the estimated oil reserves from the published accounts. Instead, he'll make his own forecasts of the likely earnings that will be made as the oil is extracted and sold. His forecasts will take account of the likely future oil price, the exchange rate, likely future tax regime, and so on.

Fundamental analysts often concentrate on a particular group of companies, or sector of the stock market – perhaps oil companies, as in the previous example, or the retailing sector, chemical manufacturers, and so on. When looking at any particular company, the analyst is likely to compare it against other companies in the same sector to see how share prices, company performance and prospects compare.

So the fundamental analyst will focus on a clutch of present and forecast statistics covering earnings, price/earnings ratios, dividend yields, net asset values per share, and so on. He will use these to establish whether a company's shares look cheap, and should therefore be bought or held, or whether they look expensive and should be sold.

The tools of the trade for the fundamental analyst are all published information about the company, such as reports and accounts, interim results, rights issue prospectuses, company announcements, and other published information, such as relevant economic statistics. The analyst will try to build up his knowledge further by visits to the companies in his charge.

Does it work?

If you choose a selection of shares in some random way – by sticking pins in the share pages of your morning newspaper, say – you'd end up with a portfolio whose performance over time would be close to the average for all shares. Professional fund managers – running unit trusts, insurance funds and pension funds – overwhelmingly favour fundamental analysis. If that method of analysis works, you would expect a fund chosen according to its recommendations to do better than the portfolio you randomly chose from your paper.

There have been numerous studies of the performance of professionally managed funds both here and in the USA. *Which?* has itself carried out some research into the performance of unit trusts and of share tipsters. The conclusions have all been very similar: professionally managed funds and tipping services are not able to produce better results than those for shares as a whole. In fact, the performance of professionally managed funds tends to be slightly worse than for the market as a whole because active buying and selling runs up dealing costs which must be charged against the funds.

The logical conclusion is that fundamental analysis is not an effective method of picking which shares will be winners.

Chartism

This method of analysis is also called **technical analysis**. It also starts with the idea that share markets tend to be efficient. The gist of the chartists' view is that since share prices fully reflect all known information about a company, the only unexplained factor in the movement of a share price is the behaviour of investors. Moreover, investors tend to act in a predictable manner – as can be seen from the study of charts of past price movements (looking just at the share price itself and also at its movements relative to the market as a whole).

Chartists try to identify price levels at which investors will be triggered to act – either in buying, or ceasing to sell shares as prices fall through the given level, or in selling or ceasing to buy shares as the price rises through some given level. There may be interim prices at which temporary buying or selling takes place. For example, a general rise in share price may be temporarily halted as some investors decide to take their profits; a general fall in prices may be temporarily pulled up as investors decide they see a good buying opportunity. Actions like these cause the formation of particular shapes in the analysts' charts – which are given intriguing names such as 'head and shoulders', 'double bottoms' and 'double tops'. If you look at a chart of historic share prices you may well identify such shapes, and they may indeed be explained by investor behaviour, but whether it is possible to accurately spot their formation without the benefit of hindsight is doubtful.

Some chartist theories have been refined to a very highly regulated form, with buying and selling being dictated by the occurrence of very precise circumstances. Other methods of chartism allow the analyst more scope for making his own judgements.

Does it work?
The research by the proponents of the Efficient Market Hypothesis suggests very strongly that past performance can't be a guide to the future movement of prices. This totally undermines the basis of chartism, with its reliance on the movement of past prices. And tests which have been carried out on a number of chartist systems have found that those systems do not work.

Beta analysis
Beta analysis is not concerned with selecting stock market winners, but looks at the degree to which different share prices vary compared with share prices as a whole. The aim is to identify shares which are consistently either affected a lot or only a little by movements in the stock market.

The **beta** of a share (not to be confused with the SEAQ category of beta stocks) is a measure of how much its rate of return is going to be affected by movements in the stock market. A beta of 1 means that the return on the share is expected to alter exactly in line with the market average. A beta greater than 1 means that the return will increase by more than the market average when the market is rising, but will also fall by more than the market average when the market is falling. For example, if a share has a beta of 1.5, it is expected to rise half as much again as the market when the market is rising. A share with a beta greater than 1 is called an *aggressive* share. A share with a beta of less than 1 is called a *defensive* share; it is expected to fall by less than the market average when the market is falling, and to rise by less than the market average when the market is rising. For example, a share with a beta of 0.5 is expected to fall by only half the amount of the market average in a falling market.

Does it work?
The beta describes a statistically observed relationship and can't therefore be 'wrong'. But the beta of a share may be expected to vary over time, so it won't necessarily be a reliable indicator of share price movement relative to the market. And, of course, beta analysis doesn't claim to be a method of choosing the shares which will be winners. It can only be an aid to choosing or rejecting the shares which may fluctuate more widely than others.

Inside information
Inside information is knowledge which is not generally available to all the investors in a market. For example, an employee in a merchant bank may know in advance of any announcement that a particular company is to be the subject of a takeover bid by another company, the director of a company will know in advance that his company will be announcing a cut in dividends. This sort of information puts the holder of it in a position where he could buy or sell shares and make a tidy profit once the information becomes generally available and absorbed into the share price.

But insider dealing is now a criminal offence, and people who make use of privileged information that they have as a result of being, say, a director, employee, contractor or adviser to a company could face fines and/or imprisonment. There have been several recent and highly publicised prosecutions for insider dealing, and it's beginning to look as if this offence could be a widespread one.

Does it work?
Possession of genuine inside information not generally available to other investors could indeed be effective if used as a basis for share dealing – but such use would be a criminal offence.

However, some so-called inside information is in fact so widely known or guessed at that the share price has already taken it into account. So when news is finally announced, there is little or no change in the share price. Other so-called inside information is nothing more than rumour, or even false information which has been planted.

Past performance

Advertisements, and investment advisers in particular, are prone to refer to past performance as an indication of the soundness of a particular investment. This is a technique commonly used with unit trusts and with insurance funds. Often a comparison will be drawn either with other trusts or funds available, or with some other investment that you're likely to have experience of – such as a building society account.

These charts and figures can look very persuasive. But, as the discussion above points out, a great deal of research has been done which strongly suggests that past performance can be no guide to the future. Many statistical surveys have been done to try to establish whether there is any link between past and future performance of funds or trusts, and no link has been found. Intuitively, this may be hard to accept – surely a good management team which has produced good results for a fund in the past should be more likely to produce good results in the future than the management team of a poorly performing fund? The research does not support this view. Do not be tempted to use past performance as a basis for your investment decisions.

Share tipping

You are bound to come across share tips – either in the columns of newspapers and specialist magazines, or from your stockbroker or other adviser. These recommendations (which tend to concentrate on tips to 'buy', more rarely on tips to 'sell') may look misleadingly successful: tipsters often pick out small companies. With these, it doesn't take many buyers to precipitate a fairly significant rise in price. So the tipped price rise may in fact be due solely to the tip itself. If this is the case, the price is likely to fall back in a few days, weeks or even months, and then resume its former course.

But as a private investor you can't normally profit from this type of short-term movement as a result of a tip. Take, for example, an influential firm of stockbrokers, who as a result of their research decide that Company X is a red-hot 'buy'. First the firm will phone the recommendation through to its major clients – institutional investors such as pension funds, insurance companies and unit trusts who have £millions to invest. Soon the news will be all around the City and within a couple of hours of that first phone call, the share price will have risen. The private investor hasn't had a look in. As for newspaper tips, you are in good company with all the other readers of the paper! In general, you'll find the share price has already moved before you can act. Even if there's still some scope for the price to rise, you may find that dealing costs eat heavily into any profit you make.

11 *Reading the financial newspapers*

First the bad news. There is next to no scope for coming across company information in a newspaper which you can act on to your immediate financial advantage.

Take, for example, news about a company's profits or about its progress (e.g. sales, contracts won, new developments). All such information has already been reflected in the share price by the time you can act – e.g. buy shares or (if it is bad news) sell them.

The same goes for buy (or more rarely sell) recommendations that you may read in the press – whether these derive from a report of recommendations made by a stockbroker, or are a newspaper tipster's own recommendations (see page 79).

On the other hand, if you follow company news over a period of time you will be equipping yourself to make sensible and informed judgements. Though unless you add what you read in the press to your own observations of companies of which you have first-hand knowledge, you are unlikely to find yourself one jump ahead of other investors.

The other main feature of financial news in the press is the page or so given over to share price information. But, as with the list of runners in the 3.40 at York, no amount of study is going to enable you to pick the winners. The primary use of share price information is to check up on the prices of shares you already own, or on the prices of shares you are keeping an eye on. But, varying with the newspaper, quite a wide range of other information may be included.

When looking up share information, you'll first have to track down your company. Company shares are normally grouped into particular sections – *Drapery and stores*, *Electricals*, *Industrials*, *Insurance*, etc. So you'll need to know the main business your company is involved in. Exactly where you'll find it varies from one newspaper to another since their categories are not exactly the same (see page 68). Overleaf, we give an example from the *Financial Times*, along with an explanation of what each figure is and what you can deduce from it.

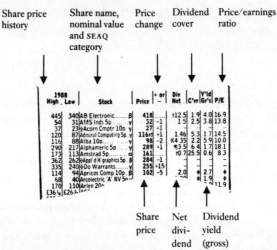

| Share price history | Share name, nominal value and SEAQ category | Price change | Dividend cover | Price/earnings ratio |

1988 High , Low	Stock	Price	+ or –	Div Net	C'yr	Y'ld Gr's	P/E
445 340	AB Electronic.......β	418	......	†12.5	1.9	4.0	16.9
54 31	AMS Inds 5p ...... γ	52	–1	1.5	2.5	3.8	13.8
37 23	½Acorn Cmptr 10p γ	27	+1				
120 87	Admiral Computing 5p. γ	116n	+1	1.46	5.3	1.7	14.5
116 88	Alba 10o........... γ	98	–2	K4 35	2.2	5.9	10.0
290 217	Alphameric 5p..... γ	289	+1	◄3.5	6.4	1.7	18.1
173 113	Amstrad 5p........ α	161	......	†0.7	25.5	0.6	8.3
362 262	Appl d H graphics 5p .β	284	–1	–	–	–	
335 240	½Do Warrants.......γ	255	+15	–	–	–	
114 94	Apricot Comp 10p. β	102	–5	2.0	♦	2.7	♦
68 40	Arcolectric 'A' NV 5p..			.on	♦	1.9	♦
170 110	Arlen 20p						◄11.9
£36¾ £26¼							

| | | Share price | Net dividend | Dividend yield (gross) | |

An example of shares in the Electricals category of the *Financial Times.*

Share price history

These columns show the highest and lowest prices for that share, during the current calendar year (from January up to Budget Day in any year, the record goes back to January of the *previous* year). Prices have been adjusted to take account of **rights issues** and **scrip issues** (see Chapter 14). The figures enable you to compare the current share price with the best (and worst) times for that share over the recent past, and check whether the price is now at a high, low or somewhere in between. With the aid of a calculator and a certain amount of homework, you could compare one share with another – to see, for example, which prices were closest to (or furthest from) their high.

Share name, nominal value and SEAQ category

Your company's name (or an abbreviated form) will be followed by the share's nominal or 'par' value (if nothing is stated, assume it is 25p). The nominal value is of no importance to you as an investor – it's done for the benefit of company law and the company's accountants. As you can see, it bears no relationship to the share's value. Symbols before the name tell you if the share does not have full Stock Exchange listing – e.g. if it is traded on the **Unlisted Securities Market**. And on the right of this column, the Greek letters α, β or γ show whether the SEAQ dealing system classes the share as an alpha, beta or gamma stock.

Share price

This is a rough guide to the price you would have to pay if buying shares (or get, if selling). Prices are usually quoted in pence up to 999p then, from £10 or more, in pounds and fractions of pounds. Usually just one price is given, which is yesterday's middle-market closing price – i.e. half-way between what buyers paid and sellers received. *The Times* gives offer *and* bid prices (i.e. a better indication of what you would pay if buying, or get if selling, respectively); this is also a very useful guide to the prevailing gap (the spread) between offer and bid prices – something that can vary widely, anything from 0.5 per cent to 10 per cent or more, depending on the company.

On its own, the share price isn't very useful (except in tracking the performance of the company). A share with a low price isn't necessarily better value than one with a high price. You need more information than price alone.

The letters 'xd' after the price mean **ex-dividend** – which means that the buyer of the shares will not get the next dividend which has been declared and is due to be paid. If there is no 'xd' after the price, you can assume that the shares would be sold **cum dividend** – that the buyer would get the next dividend.

Price change

This gives the amount the price has changed (up or down) by comparison with the previous day's middle-market closing price.

Net dividend

This shows the total dividend paid out per share for the current year – in the *Financial Times*, listed after income tax has been deducted. Some papers list gross dividends, i.e. net dividend + tax credit (see page 47). Dividends are normally paid out twice a year (the figure quoted is the total for the last 12 months). You can assume that the dividends are in pence per share, unless they are shown with a % sign – in which case they are given as a percentage of the nominal value of the shares. Various symbols – explained in a footnote – give more details about the dividend.

Dividend cover

This is the number of times the gross dividends for the last 12 months could have been paid out of the company's after-tax profits for the same period. A high figure may suggest scope for increasing dividends. A figure of less than one means that the dividends are larger than the company's earnings - i.e. the company is likely to be using profits retained from previous years to top up the dividend. Obviously, this is not a situation that could continue forever. But you would be unwise to form a view about a company's health on the basis of any one statistic such as 'dividend cover' – what really matters is the *future* flow of dividends, which no statistics are going to tell you.

Dividend yield (gross)

This shows the before-tax income from each £100 invested in the shares, based on the gross dividends for the last 12 months and the current share price quoted in the newspaper. If you're interested in investing for a high income, it's worth looking at shares with a high dividend yield. A high dividend yield may mean a high immediate income from your investment – but, of course, doesn't tell you what will happen to dividends over the *next* 12 months. It is worth bearing in mind that a high dividend yield implies that the share price is depressed, and that the company or industry is out of favour with investors – whose judgement is sometimes wrong, of course (but sometimes right).

Price/earnings ratio

The price/earnings ratio (P/E or PE for short) is the current share price divided by the most recent year's earnings per share (i.e. after-tax profits, worked out on a per share basis). The PE ratio is a measure of how cheaply you are buying the earnings made by the company. Taken in isolation, it does not tell you anything very useful, since the circumstances in different industries vary widely. But the PE ratio is much used when comparing similar companies in the same industry. If the PE ratio is high, investors in general are expressing confidence in the company. The company's earnings are low at the moment relative to the share price, but investors don't mind because they think future growth in earnings will make up for this. A low PE ratio, on the other hand, may mean that the company's profits are a solid basis for the share price – or it may mean that the share price is in the doldrums. Interpreting PE ratios and acting on them is down to you – or your adviser. Unfortunately there is no rule of thumb.

12 Company reports and accounts

A set of company reports and accounts can provide a devotee with hours of happy analysis. It takes a lot of experience to get the most out of them. And, as we have seen in Chapter 10, the company's share price will already have reflected the information given in the accounts. That said, the report and accounts are one of the basic ways of finding out about a company: what it does – and how well – what it owns and owes, and, when combined with other information, what the stock market thinks about it.

Getting hold of them

The results for companies listed on the Stock Exchange must be notified to shareholders twice yearly, and will often get reported in the press. Every Saturday the *Financial Times* publishes a list of which companies' results are due to be announced in the following week. There tends to be quite a bit of active dealing in a company's shares in the few weeks before the results are announced, as investors try to anticipate them; this explains why, when the results are actually published, little may happen to the share price (if the investors have guessed correctly). The share price may even fall if the results are worse than expected.

A few weeks after the announcement of the final results, and usually before the AGM, you should automatically be sent a copy of the report and accounts for any companies whose shares you hold.

If you're not a shareholder, you have to ask for the accounts. To do so, write either to the registrar of the company you are interested in, or to the company secretary at the registered office of the company itself. The addresses of both registrars and registered offices of companies listed on the Stock Exchange are published in a number of directories which should be available at your local reference library – for example, the Stock Exchange Official Year Book. Alternatively, you can consult the Companies' Registration Office (see page 132). A limited registered company has to file its accounts with this office. You can ask to see particular accounts (at a cost of £1 per company for personal callers, £3 per document by post), but since company accounts take some time to reach the Office what you see may be out of date. The magazine *Investors Chronicle* will also send copies of recent (up to three weeks old) reports and accounts to readers on request (write to PO Box EL/10/A, FREEPOST, *The Investors Chronicle*, London EC4B 4QJ).

Pit and Pendulum plc
& subsidiary companies

consolidated profit-and-loss account
for the year ended
31 December 1987

	Notes	1987 £000	1986 £000
Turnover	2	25,195	22,507
Net operating costs	3	23,313	21,263
Operating profit		1,882	1,244
Share of associated companies' profits		18	7
Other income	6	122	252
		2,022	1,503
Interest payable	7	672	710
Profit on ordinary activities before taxation		1,350	793
Taxation on profit on ordinary activities	8	478	454
Profit on ordinary activities after taxation		872	339
Minority interests		230	156
Profit on ordinary activities before extraordinary items		592	183
Extraordinary items	9	136	18
Profit for the financial year		728	201
Dividends	10	109	22
Retained profit transferred to reserves		619	179
Earnings per Ordinary Share	11	7.28p	1.80p
Statement of retained profits			
Retained profits brought forward		1,413	1,325
Retained profits for the year		619	179
Goodwill written off		–	(13)
Capitalisation of reserves in a subsidiary		–	(78)
Transfer to other reserves	21	(74)	–
Retained profits carried forward		1,958	1,413

consolidated balance sheet

Fixed assets	Notes	£000	1987 £000	£000	1986 £000
Tangible assets	12		5,408		4,490
Investments	13		129		130
			5,537		4,620
Current assets Stocks	14	6,315		6,429	
Debtors	15	6,348		5,821	
Cash at bank and in hand		2,614		1,891	
		15,277		14,141	
Creditors: amounts falling due within one year	16	8,593		8,378	
Net current assets			6,684		5,763
Total assets less current liabilities			12,221		10,383
Creditors amounts falling due after more than one year	16	2,023		1,183	
Provisions for liabilities and charges	18	413		872	
			2,436		2,055
			9,785		8,328
Capital and reserves Called up share capital	20		2,420		2,420
Share premium			506		506
Revaluation reserve	21		930		874
Other reserves	21		1,289		952
Profit and loss account	22		1,958		1,413
Shareholders' funds			7,103		6,165
Minority interests			2,682		2,163
			9,785		8,328

Approved by the Board of Directors on 21 May 1988

Directors
M. F. Pit
J. R. Pendulum

However, particularly since the government privatisations, some companies – including TSB and British Telecom – have complained about the costs of sending reports and accounts to their millions of shareholders. It's possible that the law may be changed so that companies can send a simplified version to private shareholders who don't ask for the full set.

What they show

How companies present their accounts differs widely. But they all break down into a number of separate parts.

The chairman's and directors' reports come first, and give a useful overview of the company's activities during the past year and expectations for the future. These reports aren't always just a propaganda exercise – they can give warning of a change in direction with which you may not agree. The directors' report also gives information on the company's shares owned by individual directors, which may give you a feeling for what they think about the company. Somewhere you'll also find the auditors' report, which will tell you if they think the accounts give a true and fair picture of the company's finances. If they don't think so, watch out.

The background to the reports is shown in the *profit-and-loss account* and the *balance sheet*. The profit-and-loss account tells you how much income the business has earned, what has gone out in the way of expenses and taxation, and therefore what the after-tax profits are. Then it shows the amount the company intends to pay out to shareholders in the form of dividends. It won't usually pay out all its profits – some will be kept back in the form of 'retained earnings' and transferred across to the balance sheet in the form of 'reserves' used to finance expansion of the business, say, or to guard against a rainy day.

The balance sheet shows what the company's financial position is at a particular moment in time (the end of the accounting year). So you need to take the timing into account – the stocks of a retailing company may be particularly high just before Christmas, say. The balance sheet starts off by totting up what the company owns – its assets – divided into fixed assets including plant and machinery, and current assets such as stocks, money the company is owed, and cash. Then its debts – or liabilities – are shown, divided into 'current' liabilities such as short-term borrowing and money the company owes its suppliers, and longer-term liabilities such as loans repayable after more than a year. Liabilities are deducted from assets to end up with net assets (or net liabilities). The balance sheet finishes up by showing how those net assets (or liabilities) are financed – for example, by capital put in by shareholders and reserves transferred from the profit-and-loss account.

You'll also come across a *statement of source and application of funds*. This explains in more detail where the cash has come from, and where it has gone, for example in payments to shareholders, tax and increased funds for a particular purpose. It gives you some feel for whether the company's cash flow (money actually received less money spent) is satisfactory.

Finally, don't neglect any notes to the accounts. They tell you how the accounts have been prepared, and you may come across some interesting information, for example how (and when) company properties have been valued.

What to look for

The figures in the report and accounts may not mean too much on their own: the art is to compare them with the same figures for previous years and other, similar companies. Important figures to look for on the profit-and-loss account and balance sheet for Pit and Pendulum plc on pages 86 and 87 include:

- **After-tax profits** Divide by the number of shares issued, and you'll come up with the company's *earnings per share* (this figure must be shown in the accounts for companies listed on the Stock Exchange). For Pit and Pendulum plc, which has 10 million ordinary shares and whose accounts are shown on page 86, the earnings per share would be £728,000 divided by 10 million – 7.28p per share. If you compare earnings per share for the latest year with the same figure for previous years (this, plus much other useful information, is shown on company information cards published by Extel Financial Ltd – try your library) you can measure how the company has grown over the years. And you'll need to know earnings per share to work out the **price/earnings ratio** (see page 84).
- **Amount of gross dividends** Divide the after-tax profits by this figure to find the dividend cover (see page 83). For Pit and Pendulum plc, the cover would be £728,000 divided by £109,000, i.e. 6.7. In other words the company earned 6.7 times as much as it paid out in dividends.
- **Net asset value** This is assets minus liabilities, i.e. what the company is worth. It is important in a number of situations. For example, by working out the *net assets per share* for Pit and Pendulum plc (9.785 million divided by 10 million – 97.8p) you can see that if E.A.Poe Holdings offers to take them over for 100p per share, it's not much of an offer. The net assets per share are useful for working out what's backing your shares if the company decided to close down (though in a forced sale the assets may not fetch their full value). When compared with the share price, this figure can also help you judge what the stock

market thinks about the company (particularly investment trust companies – see page 20). For example, if Pit and Pendulum plc were trading on the stock market for 147p a share – 50p more than the net assets per share – you could see that investors were willing to pay more for their shares than their intrinsic value (called trading at a **premium**; the opposite would be trading at a **discount**).

Beware

Not all may be what it seems in a particular set of accounts. Accounting conventions may mean that information is not always presented in the most useful way for investors. For example, a company which takes over another company might include the whole of its acquisition's profits for the year – even if it bought it only a month or so before the year-end. The notes to the accounts may throw some light on such points.

Section III

Owning shares

13 *How to do well out of takeovers*

If you own shares, one of your companies may be faced with a takeover bid. In a recent *Which?* survey, nearly a quarter of people who owned shares had been faced with a takeover or merger in the previous five years.

Takeovers can be very lucrative for shareholders in the target company, but it's sometimes tricky to work out exactly what to do and when to do it. So if you find yourself in this position, the first rule is to stay abreast of what's going on. The financial press should keep you up to date with any new developments. The bigger the company, the more detailed newspaper reports are likely to be. A stockbroker should be able to inform and advise you, too.

Why takeovers happen

The object of a takeover is simple. The bidding company wants to get control of the target company. It can do this by acquiring a bare majority (i.e. 51 per cent) of the target company's shares. But, in order to exercise effective authority, it will almost certainly want to get more than this.

The reasons behind a takeover are not always so clear. The bidding company will probably insist that it can do a much better job of running the target company than the current directors. The target company may well disagree, and, as you'll see, some bids are so fraught with claim and counter-claim that the truth can be difficult to discern. Perhaps the most common reason for a takeover is that the bidding company wants to increase its earnings. It works like this. If a bidder with 50 million issued shares earns £5 million after tax, its earnings are 10p per share. Suppose it takes over a smaller company with 30 million shares, making £5 million profit. The result of the takeover will be a single company, with 80 million shares, making profits of £10 million. The new company's earnings per share are 12.5p. So our bidder has increased its earnings by 25 per cent. Some companies, for example Hanson Trust, which started small, have grown dramatically by a shrewd programme of takeovers.

What happens in a takeover

The rules that govern takeovers are extremely complex. We'll come across some of them in this chapter. The Panel on Takeovers and Mergers – part of the City's system of self-regulation – referees takeovers and makes sure that the rules are obeyed.

Every takeover is different, but they tend to follow a similar pattern. The bidding company starts off by buying as many shares as possible without alerting the market to what's going on. Once it has acquired five per cent of the target company it must declare its shareholding. This may be accompanied by a statement to the effect that it is buying shares in the company purely as an investment for the future and that the thought of a takeover is the furthest thing from its mind.

At this point, rumours of a takeover bid may start to circulate. The rumours may be reported in the financial press. The share price will start to rise as investors buy into the target company in the hope of rich pickings, should a takeover bid be made.

As an alternative to this approach, the bidding company may make what is melodramatically known as a 'dawn raid'. This means that they try to buy large numbers of shares in a short space of time. At one time a bidding company could, in this way, buy enough shares in the target company to gain effective control before the target company had time to mount an effective defence. But in 1980 the Panel on Takeovers and Mergers ruled that once a company has bought 14.9 per cent of the target company in this way, it has to stop for a week.

By now, the company's shares will probably have risen substantially, and shareholders might be tempted to sell their shares in the market and take the profits. You should think twice before doing this. It's certainly true that if the bid fails to materialise, the share price could fall back. But the company, having been considered as a possible takeover target, may continue to look attractive to investors, so the share price could stay high. And, of course, another bidder may appear.

The bidding company continues to buy shares in the target company until it has built up a stake of 30 per cent. At this point it must stop and make a formal offer to the remaining shareholders. You'll probably first find out the terms of the offer from reading the financial press.

Shareholders in the target company will shortly afterwards be sent the offer document. This will set out the terms of the offer, and the closing date for acceptance. You don't need to worry too much about the closing date – most bids are extended and bidders are usually quite happy to take acceptances after the official closing date. But if the bidder has offered a cash alternative, this may not be available after the closing date.

The takeover bid may attract the attention of other companies, who suddenly realise that the target company has been undervalued in the past. A second bidder may enter the fray. The new bidder may be a 'white knight' – welcomed and encouraged by the target company. Alternatively, the bidder may be a 'black knight' – just as unwelcome to the target company as the original bidder.

Whatever the colour of the knight, the share price will almost certainly start to rise again. If it wants to stay in the race, the company which made the original bid will have to increase its offer. Don't despair if you've accepted the original offer and a better one comes along. In most cases (although it depends on the exact terms of the offer), you can withdraw your original acceptance and take advantage of the higher offer, providing the offer hasn't gone 'unconditional'. This happens when the bidder has acquired the proportion of the shares (usually 50 per cent) specified in the offer document. Once a bid is unconditional, there's no point in holding out. Your shares are no longer in such demand. The bidder has gained control of the company and you'll probably find it difficult to sell your shares in the market. Accept the offer. In any case, once the bidder has acquired 90 per cent of the shares in the target company, it can compulsorily acquire the rest.

Deciding what to do

What you really want to know is how much the bidding company is prepared to pay for your shares. It may offer cash, or shares in the bidding company, or a mixture of both. If the offer is for shares in the bidding company, you need to decide whether or not you really want the shares. If you don't, and there is no cash alternative, you could sell your shares in the market. If you do this, in most cases you'll get slightly less than the offer price.

It's worth bearing in mind that if you accept cash, you could be liable for capital gains tax (CGT) at the time – how much depends on how long you've owned the shares. But if you opt for shares, you won't have to pay CGT. If you've owned your shares for a long time, you may well be sitting on a large capital gains tax liability – so you would do better to accept shares rather than cash.

You may also get a letter from the directors of the target company, recommending that you accept the offer. The directors might do this because they genuinely believe that the takeover is in the best interests of their company, or they might just be bowing to the inevitable. Where the target company agrees, this is known as an agreed bid or a merger. Take your time before following the directors' advice. It's far from unusual for another company to appear on the scene with a better offer and start the share price moving again.

Contested bids

Shareholders can expect to see a healthy profit on an agreed bid, but contested bids tend to be still more lucrative. If the target company decides to try to fight off the bid, the directors will make their views known, probably in the press and certainly by contacting shareholders. They will probably denounce the bid as inadequate and paint a rosy picture of the target company's prospects. They may believe what they're saying; on the other hand, it's not unknown for directors to be motivated by the possibility of losing their jobs, should the bid succeed.

If the bid is contested, you can expect to be bombarded with letters and possibly even telephone calls from both sides. In the Burtons/Debenhams battle, some shareholders were sent a video recording encouraging them to accept the offer. The bidder may attack the target company's record and will explain that it would do a far better job. The target company will defend its record. If the company has been in the doldrums of late (as is often the case with takeover targets) it will try to persuade you that the lean period has come to an end. In turn, it will attack the record of the bidding company.

In a really big takeover battle like Burtons' bid for Debenhams and the three-way struggle between Argyll, Distillers and Guinness, the companies involved may place advertisements in newspapers to put their case. This is less common now than it used to be, because the Takeover Panel keeps a close eye on such adverts and has, in the past, had to step in to prevent companies from using misleading information in their advertisements and in circulars to shareholders.

Try not to pay too much attention to the propaganda you'll receive from both sides. The financial press will probably be more helpful. They regularly publish a list of acceptances, so you can see how the bid is progressing. The papers should also be able to indicate whether the big institutions, the insurance companies and pension funds who decide the fate of most takeovers, are planning to sell up or hold on to their shares. In practice, the institutions tend to favour accepting bids, to take the short-term profits.

In the face of all this, what should your strategy be? Wait as long as you can before accepting any offer. Under the Takeover Panel's rules, the first offer period lasts for between 21 and 60 days from the date when the offer document was posted. The bidding company can increase the offer several times during that period if it wants to. But shareholders always get 14 days to consider any proposals, so a company can't make a new offer after the forty-sixth day.

So you've got plenty of time in which to make up your mind. You can afford to wait and see how the market reacts. The target company often manages to convince investors that the offer price was too low. If this happens, investors will expect a new and higher bid. They'll continue buying or holding the target company's shares so its share price will remain at a higher level in the market than the bidding company has offered. The offer will have to be increased to stand any chance of success.

Some target companies manage to mount such a vigorous defence that they persuade the institutions that they'd do better to give their support to the existing board of directors. In 1986 Woolworth managed to fight off a bid from Dixons, the consumer electronics chain. Dixons were thriving and had seen their share price rocket over the previous 18 months. Woolworth were trying to shed their somewhat dowdy and down-market image by reorganising their high-street shops. Dixons tried to persuade Woolworth's shareholders that they would do a much better job of running the company. But Woolworth's share price stayed well above the original offer as Woolworth's board successfully convinced shareholders that their programme of reorganisation was working. Even Dixons' increased bid failed to convince the institutions that they would improve the company's fortunes. The existing directors maintained control of the company.

Failed bids

Don't be too disappointed if the bid fails. You may miss out on the short-term profits, but it sometimes pays to take a longer view. If the management has become lethargic and complacent, a takeover bid may shake them up. A bid may also convince other investors that the company is a worthwhile proposition. So you may find yourself holding shares in a much more attractive company.

Occasionally a bid may be referred to the Monopolies and Mergers Commission (MMC). The MMC has to decide if the bid is against the public interest. It's not always easy to know what criteria they will use. Nowadays, however, they tend to ban only those bids that might make the market less competitive. GEC's bid for Plessey fell foul of the MMC for this reason. When a bid is referred to the MMC, it automatically lapses. If the MMC decides to allow it to go ahead, the bidding company can, if it wishes, renew the offer. But the MMC takes a long time to come to a decision – six months or more in some cases. So even if a bid is allowed to proceed, the moment may have passed and the bidding company may no longer be interested. The target company will, in any case, take advantage of the breathing space afforded by a referral to build up its defences to the bid. Some bidders make their offers conditional on the bid not being referred to the MMC. If rumours start to circulate of a referral to the MMC, it may be time to sell your shares in the market.

But a referral needn't necessarily kill a bid off. Some companies have found ways around it. The Guinness bid for Distillers was in danger of being referred to the MMC because it might have led to too many brands of whisky being held by one company. Guinness avoided a referral by promising that if the bid were successful, it would sell off some of the whisky brands. It eventually managed to take Distillers over.

Investing for takeovers

Clearly the best way to make money out of a takeover bid is by getting in at the ground floor. So how do you spot a company that's ripe to be taken over? You want a company that is basically sound but is going through a lean period. Look through the share listings in newspapers. If you spot a company that's not doing as well as others in the sector, try to find out why. It may be a company which has fallen back because of over-expansion. It may have too much of its capital locked away in land or plant; a company taking it over could realise those assets. Perhaps it is burdened with inefficient management. Or a basically successful company may be held back because a part of it is doing badly.

Watch out for signs of interest from other companies. As we have seen, potential bidders often signal their interest by taking a share stake in the company. This is usually reported in the financial press. Bid rumours, too, often make the newspapers. But be prepared for disappointment. Even though the signs are right, the bid may never materialise.

14 Rights issues and scrip issues

Rights issues

A company makes a **rights issue** as a way of raising more money by asking its shareholders to buy more shares. It may want to do this to expand the business, for example, or even to bail itself out if it's in financial difficulties.

In a rights issue, all existing shareholders are sent a provisional letter of allotment offering them the right to buy new shares in the company. These new shares are allotted in proportion to the number each shareholder already owns. In a 'one-for-three' rights issue, for example, you'll be offered the right to buy one new share for each three you already own.

The price of the new shares is fixed when the rights issue is announced – and it will normally be lower than the market price of the existing shares to make the new shares look like an attractive proposition. However, the value of your existing shares will fall as soon as the rights issue has been announced, as a result of new shares becoming available at below the market price. The price that the old shares falls to is known as the **ex-rights price**.

You can easily work out the value of your existing shares using the following Example:

Example

Suppose you own 600 shares in *Expand plc*, which are trading at 120p when a one-for-three rights issue at 100p is announced.

You have 600 old shares at 120p each £720

You have rights to 200 new shares (one-for-three) at 100p each £200

So your total new shareholding would be 800 shares worth £920

In theory, your shares are now worth 115p each (i.e. £920 divided by 800); this is the calculated ex-rights price. In practice, the ex-rights price could be higher or lower than this, depending on the view investors take of the company's prospects – you can check the price in a newspaper.

You can sell your rights to the new shares, should you decide you don't want to take them up. The sums on page 100 take you through the calculations – you'll find that the value of the rights to the new shares *plus* the value of your old shares at the ex-rights price *equals* the value of your old shares before the rights issue was made.

After a rights issue is announced, you normally have two or three weeks before the *rights call* is due. This is the last day you can exercise your rights – i.e. buy some or all of the new shares. Alternatively, of course, you may decide you don't want any of them. In the meantime the market price of the shares (which is now the ex-rights price) may fluctuate. It will rise if investors are optimistic about the company's prospects. In this case the value of the rights – called the **premium** – will increase, because the difference between the market price of the existing shares and the price of the rights issue will have increased.

If, on the other hand, investors are pessimistic about the company's prospects, the market price of the shares will fall. The difference between this and the price of the rights issue shares will narrow – and may even disappear altogether, so wiping out the value of the rights.

Your view of the company's prospects will determine whether or not you take up any of your rights issue shares:

If you're pessimistic about the company's prospects, you'll probably want to reduce your investment in it, so don't buy any of the rights issue shares. But you'll still have to get rid of your unused rights and there are two ways of doing this:

1 Pick what you believe is a good time to sell during the period up to the rights call, and send the provisional letter of allotment (which offered you the rights) to your stockbroker – after signing the **form of renunciation** (form X) on the back. Ask him to sell your rights – which are called **nil-paid rights** – to the extra shares. Dealings are for cash, so you should get your money promptly. But you'll have to pay normal rates of stockbrokers' commission, and this can prove expensive as you're likely to have to pay the minimum charge.

2 Alternatively, you could do nothing – and simply wait until the company sells off all the unused nil-paid rights, including yours, in the market, and pays you your share of the proceeds. UK companies always do this, though foreign companies may not. This second method is cheaper – you still have to pay commission, but only at the (lower) rate which applies to large-scale sales. However, you *might* have done better by selling the rights earlier – your decision will depend on what you think will happen to the ex-rights share price during the period up to the rights call.

Whichever method you use, don't forget to alter your share records.

If you're optimistic about the company's prospects, you may want to increase your investment in it. Provided the rights issue price is below the ex-rights market price of the shares, send off a cheque shortly before the rights call is due for as many of the new shares as you want to buy. (If the rights issue price is *above* the market price, don't buy any.) There are no charges or Stamp Duty when you take up a rights issue, so you simply pay the price at which the shares are offered. If you don't buy all the new shares to which you're entitled, see opposite for what to do about the unused rights.

Alternatively, you may simply want to maintain the same investment in the company, in which case you should buy some of the new rights issue shares. (If you don't buy any, you'll actually be *reducing* your investment in the company, as the price of your existing shares will have fallen after the rights issue was announced.) See opposite for what to do about the unused rights to shares you haven't taken up. Again, don't send off your cheque until shortly before the rights call is due – and check, before you do, that the market price hasn't fallen so much that it's now below the rights issue price (if it is, don't buy).

To work out exactly how many rights issue shares you'll need to buy to maintain the same investment in the company, as well as how to work out the ex-rights price and the value of your rights, see page 100. And, again, don't forget to alter your share records.

Scrip issues

As a company grows, its share price increases; but it may grow so much that it's felt to be too unwieldy to be traded easily on the stock market. In these circumstances, the company may make a scrip issue (also called a bonus, capitalisation or free issue).

In a scrip issue, all shareholders are given – free – new shares in the company in proportion to the number they already own. In a 'one-for-three' scrip issue, for example, you'll be given one new share for every three you already own.

However, because these new shares are free, no extra money is coming into the company, so the share price must fall in direct proportion to the number of new shares issued. In a one-for-three scrip issue, for example, the price will fall so that four shares are worth the same as three used to be; see page 101 for how this is calculated.

Working out the sums for rights issues

This is easiest by very simple algebra. To work out the expected ex-rights price, the algebra is as follows:

Shareholders are offered the right to buy **a** new shares for each **b** old shares; **c** is the price the old shares were trading at before the rights issue, and **d** is the price per share at which the rights are offered. You would then expect the ex-rights price to be:

$$\frac{(b \times c) + (a \times d)}{b + a}$$

Multiply what's in the brackets first, then add the two answers together, then divide by the total of **b** plus **a**.

With Expand plc (see page 97), there was a one-for-three rights issue at 100p, with the company's shares trading at 120p before the rights issue. You would expect the ex-rights price of the shares to be:

$$\frac{(3 \times 120) + (1 \times 100)}{3 + 1} = 115p$$

The value of the nil-paid rights – your rights to the extra shares – is the ex-rights price minus **d** (the price at which the rights are offered). So with Expand plc, the expected value of the nil-paid rights would be 115p − 100p = 15p per share (but could go higher or lower, depending on what investors think of the company's prospects, and therefore what happens to the ex-rights price of the shares).

If you want to maintain the same investment in the company, you'll need to work out how many unused rights to sell in order to pay for the rights issue shares that you take up – so that it all balances out. This is how to work it out:

e is the ex-rights price of the shares (take the most up to date price from a newspaper, not the one you calculated); **f** is the number of rights issue shares you've been allocated; and **d** is the price per share at which the rights are offered. The number of rights issue shares to buy is:

$$\frac{(e - d) \times f}{e}$$

Subtract **d** from **e** first, then multiply the answer by **f**, then divide the total by **e**.

Suppose, for example, that the current ex-rights price of Expand plc shares is 110p. You were allocated 2,000 rights issue shares at 100p. If you want to maintain roughly the same investment in the company, you should buy:

$$\frac{(110 - 100) \times 2,000}{110} = 182 \text{ shares}$$

This would cost you 182 × 100p = £182; and the sale of the unused 1,818 rights at 110 − 100 = 10p each would bring you in £181.80 (less commission).

The new, lower share price is supposed to be more attractive to investors, but otherwise a scrip issue is simply a book-keeping exercise. It doesn't affect the total value of your shareholding in the company – you just end up with more, but cheaper, shares. Don't forget, though, to alter your share records to show the new number of shares you own and the notional price you bought them at.

Working out the sums for scrip issues

Again, this is easiest by very simple algebra.

Shareholders are given **a** new shares for each **b** shares already owned; **c** is the price the shares were trading at before the scrip issue. You would then expect the share price **after** the scrip issue to be:

$$\frac{\mathbf{b} \times \mathbf{c}}{\mathbf{b} + \mathbf{a}}$$

Multiply **b** by **c** first, then divide by the total of **b** plus **a**.

Suppose a one-for-three scrip issue is announced and that the shares were trading at 480p before the announcement. You'd expect the share price after the scrip issue to be:

$$\frac{3 \times 480}{3 + 1} = 360p$$

If, say, you owned 300 shares originally, the value of your shareholding before the scrip issue was 300 × 480p = £1,440 worth of shares. After the scrip issue, you have 400 shares, but each one has gone down to only three-quarters of its original value. You now have 400 × 360p = £1,440 worth of shares in the company – so your total investment is unchanged.

When you alter your share records, use the same formula – but using the price you *originally* paid for the shares at **c** – to work out the 'notional' price at which you bought the shares. So, for example, if you'd originally bought the shares at 240p, the notional price would be:

$$\frac{3 \times 240}{3 + 1} = 180p$$

15 *Annual general meetings*

When you become a shareholder, you get a stake in the company and acquire the right to attend the company's annual general meeting (AGM) and any other general meetings it may hold.

Along with your annual report and accounts you will probably receive a notice stating the date, time and place of the meeting. By law, a company must normally hold an AGM every calendar year, with not more than 15 months between each, and shareholders have to be given at least 21 days' notice. Sometimes there are 'class meetings', confined to the shareholders owning one particular class of shares, e.g. preference shares.

The purpose of an annual general meeting is (ostensibly) to take business decisions requiring the approval of the shareholders. In fact, it's the occasion when the company's board answers to the shareholders for its stewardship. So don't just throw your notice of the meeting in the bin. An AGM can range from a very dull public relations exercise, with all the items on the agenda going through unopposed, to (occasionally) a fiery session with angry shareholders raising awkward matters with the directors. Whichever type it turns out to be, it gives you the chance to see who is running the company, and to ask them questions. There may also be some perks attached – many companies give shareholders a free lunch, or some of the company's products, if they attend the meeting (see Chapter 16).

If, for some reason, you can't get to the AGM but would like to make your views known, you can do so by appointing a proxy (who need not be a shareholder) to attend and vote in polls on your behalf. It's quite usual for shareholders to appoint the Chairman of the meeting as their proxy. A notice of your right to appoint a proxy should accompany the notice of the meeting, and if you do want to appoint one you should write to notify the company. Your notification must reach them at least 48 hours before the meeting.

Even if you miss the meeting and don't appoint a proxy, you must, by law, be allowed to inspect the minutes of the meeting, free of charge, at the company's registered office.

What happens at the meeting

The meeting may well start with a statement from the chairman. You will then probably be asked to:

- Approve the company's audited report and accounts.
- Approve the election or re-election of directors (depending on company rules, a number of them may be obliged to put themselves up for re-election on a regular basis).
- Approve the appointment of auditors for the following year.
- Approve the size and payment of the final dividend.

You may also be asked to approve other matters, for example:

- Give the directors the right to issue new shares without further consultation with the shareholders.
- Approve the directors' pay.
- Approve a staff incentive scheme.

The agenda is fixed by the board of directors but may include points raised by shareholders (see below).

There are two methods of voting. Any issue first has to be voted on by a show of hands: one person, one vote. Depending on the results of that vote, the chairman can then move on to a poll using voting papers. For this vote, you get one vote per share (in fact you may be asked to take part in a postal ballot about the company's affairs at any time – not just at the AGM). Most decisions can be passed by a simple majority of the shareholders who vote. But, by law, 'extraordinary' or 'special resolutions' on matters such as changing the company name or voluntarily winding-up the company require a three-quarters' majority of the total votes cast.

Shareholders' rights

Shareholders have a number of rights when it comes to meetings. They can:

- Put forward a resolution to be voted on at the AGM. This requires the signature of either shareholders with at least five per cent of the voting rights between them, or of at least one hundred shareholders who between them hold share capital of £10,000.
- Prepare a statement of not more than 1,000 words relating to matters to be voted on at the next AGM, and insist that the company circulates it

to all shareholders. However, the authors have to pay for it, not the
company, and the company can ask the courts for permission to refuse
if it considers the shareholders to be abusing their rights in order to
cause needless publicity. They also have to send it to the company at
least six weeks before the meeting, and it must be supported by the
same number of shareholders as for putting forward a resolution.

- Call for (the technical term is 'requisition') an extraordinary general
meeting (see below). This requires the signatures of members with at
least 10 per cent of the issued share capital with voting rights. If the
directors don't act within 21 days of the requisition, then shareholders
with at least half of the total voting rights are entitled to hold the
meeting themselves, with any reasonable costs reimbursed by the
company, providing they do so within three months of the requisition.

- Raise other points in the 'any other business' part of the meeting.

Extraordinary general meetings

These provide the company – or shareholders – with an opportunity to
discuss special matters at any time, e.g. the voluntary winding-up of the
company. They are run like an AGM, except that only 14 days' notice
usually has to be sent to shareholders, and some of the resolutions likely to
be discussed will need a three-quarters majority of favourable votes.

16 *Shareholders' perks*

Many companies offer perks – often called 'concessions' or 'benefits' – to their shareholders. The argument goes that perks may help, even if just a little, to support the price of a share, making it easier for a company to raise money in a rights issue (see page 97) and more difficult for the company to be taken over. Also, in a contested takeover bid (see page 94) small private investors, mindful of their perks, may be more loyal to the company than the institutions (insurance companies, pension funds and so on) who look to the immediate profits they may make. Discounts may cost a company little if it is selling to people, the shareholders, who would not otherwise have bought its products. And perks may help to promote a positive image of the company.

Shareholders' concessions, though seductive, should rarely be taken into account when you are working out which shares to buy. Most perks are fairly small, but even a good discount needs careful consideration. For instance, Barratt Developments offers a discount of £500 for each £25,000 or part of £25,000 spent on buying a new home. An £80,000 new home would attract a discount of £2,000. So, as a shareholder, you could benefit from quite a handsome discount; but you'd have to do some careful sums to see whether the discount should be part of your decision to invest in Barratt in the first place.

Not all shareholders will be eligible for a company's benefits. There are two common restrictions. You may have to hold a minimum number of shares; and you may have to hold them for a certain period of time before you qualify. Many companies, though, do not impose these restrictions. You could then buy just one share in order to qualify for the perk. However, it may be difficult to find a broker willing to act for you, and acquiring just one share (or even a minimum holding costing a few hundred pounds) could be expensive with current minimum commissions standing at around £20 or £25. If the perk is offered by a small company whose shares are not often traded, there will probably be a wide spread between the **bid** and **offer price** (see page 42) so the shares will have to perform quite well if a profit is to be made when they are sold. And a final word of warning. If a company finds its share register being swollen by large numbers of small shareholders seeking perks, the perks could be withdrawn, or a minimum holding might be introduced or increased.

How do you get your perks? They come in a number of ways. You may get them if you attend the AGM, e.g. a sample of groceries. More commonly, vouchers or forms authorising your discount will come with the annual report. Or you may be sent a shareholder's discount card (perhaps like a credit card in appearance) as soon as your name has been entered on the register of shareholders. Some companies don't automatically send out a discount card, and it will be up to you to write to the company secretary to claim it. Sometimes, you have to indicate at the point of sale that you are a shareholder and claim your discount. Your entitlement will then be checked on the register of shareholders. For instance, one holiday company has a space on its booking form to make a claim. One point to remember: you won't be eligible for the benefits until your shareholding has been registered, and this can take several weeks.

It is doubtful whether most perks can be seriously considered as part of the return on an investment. So are they worth having in themselves? The goods and services on offer must compete on quality. They must compete on price even after the discount. And they must compete on convenience. (For instance, a voucher with the annual report may not be much use to you if it has to be used by a certain date.) Don't forget to check whether there is a maximum on the total discount available – there usually is.

Two stockbrokers publish lists of companies offering shareholders' perks. Send a *large* stamped (23p), addressed envelope to Kleinwort Grieveson Investment Management Ltd, PO Box 191, 10 Fenchurch Street, London EC3M 3LB, Tel: 01-623 8000, or contact Seymour, Pierce, Butterfield Ltd, 10 Old Jewry, London EC2R 8EA, Tel: 01-628 4981 (who make a nominal charge for their list).

17 Record-keeping

The documents you should keep

Normally, whenever you buy or sell shares you will be sent a **contract note** from the stockbroker giving details of:

- What shares they are
- The number of shares you have bought or sold
- The price per share at which they have been bought or sold
- Details of all the charges (commission and – where they apply – Stamp Duty and any levy)
- If you are buying: the net cost of the shares to you, after deducting all charges. Or if you are selling: the net proceeds, after deducting all charges.

The contract note is evidence that you have bought (or sold) the shares, and at what price. You may need it as proof if the share certificate fails to appear – unlikely but not absolutely impossible. And you may also need it for the taxman – at the time (possibly many years ahead) when your capital gain or capital loss on the shares comes to be worked out and argued over. So you should keep all contract notes in a safe place. And you should aim to keep them indefinitely – or, if space for your records is limited, at least for six years *after* you have disposed of all shares in that company.

A few weeks – or sometimes longer – after buying shares, you are sent the **share certificate** for those shares. The same applies if you have sold part of a shareholding: you will receive a share certificate for the balance of shares that you still own. Share certificates, too, should be kept in a safe place, but accessible: you must be able to find them when you want to sell the shares. Moreover, if you mislay them you will find them very troublesome to replace.

When you buy a new issue of shares, you will not be sent a contract note but a **letter of allotment** (or letter of acceptance). Eventually, this will be exchanged for a share certificate, but in the meantime you should keep it carefully – it is evidence that shares have been allocated to you, and of how much you have paid. It will also tell you when the next instalment (if there is one) is due.

You should also keep all the tax vouchers that come with your dividends in case the taxman needs to see them (see Chapter 6).

The records you should make

There are two types of records that you need to keep:

- Company-by-company records
- Records of your portfolio of shares – i.e. all your shares, taken together – as a check on how they (and you) are doing.

Company-by-company records

You should keep records of all the shares you buy and sell – and of the dividends they pay you. Only proper records will keep you out of trouble with the taxman *and* enable you to make sensible investment decisions.

For instance, records of buying and selling prices, and of dividends, will give you the information you need for filling in your tax return. It can also enable you to check on how each of your shares is doing.

On page 110 we suggest the headings under which you should record information about each company's shares in which you invest (start a separate sheet for each company). And we give an example of how a purchase of 2,000 Laserwear plc shares – and the subsequent sale of 1,250 of them – should be filled in.

Most of the headings are self-explanatory, but here are a few tips on what you need to fill in, and why.

Column D asks for the total cost of each lot of shares you own (including all charges); and **column J** asks for the proceeds (after all charges) from the sale of those lots of shares. These are the figures that matter most to you (and, if you have to pay capital gains tax, to the taxman).

If you buy a new issue of shares and pay by instalments, make a note of the dates by which the instalments have to be paid. And increase the total cost of the shares (**D**) when you pay each instalment.

If you sell *less* than a full amount of a shareholding, cross out the original *number of shares bought* (**column B**), and replace it with the *same* number as you are selling (from **column H**). Then write down an entirely *new* entry for the number of shares which you still have – i.e. the original figure **B** minus **H** (the number sold) – but giving it the original date when you bought the shares. In both cases, adjust the cost of the shares (**column D**) to reflect the revised number of shares in **column B**.

If you buy the same company's shares at different times, give each lot of shares a separate entry. When you come to sell the shares, this will help you work out any capital gains tax (see Chapter 6).

Do tick off **column E** (*share certificate received?*), and make a note of the (secure) place where you keep the certificates – they are easy to mislay.

You could also use this column to record the number of the share certificate.

If you get a scrip issue of shares, cross out the original *number of shares bought* (**B**), and replace it with the new total of shares which you now have (original number plus those in the scrip issue). Make a brief note of the details in **column F** – e.g. '2 for 1 scrip', and date.

If there's a rights issue, things are a little more complicated. *If you do not take up any of the rights*, subtract the cash from the sale of the rights from the original cost of the shares, and make this the new entry in **column D**. *If you take up all of the rights*, add what you pay for the rights shares to the original cost of the shares, and make this the new entry for **D**; and at the same time, add the number of extra shares to the original number of shares, and make this the new entry in **column B**. *If you take up part of the rights*, you will have to carry out *both* the operations above, one after the other. Make a brief note of the details in **column F** – e.g. '3 for 1 rights, all taken up' and date.

With a takeover or merger, it is probably easiest to treat it as a sale, and start afresh with a new entry for the company's shares. *But from the taxman's point of view the new shares will be in the same position as the old unless you also receive some cash.*

Remember that the gain or loss (**columns K** or **L**) are almost certainly not the *taxable* gain or loss. Taxable gains are likely to be *less*, capital losses (for tax purposes) *greater* – see capital gains tax in Chapter 6.

For each company you should also record the dividends as you receive them. For each dividend you need the net dividend, tax credit, and gross dividend (net dividend plus tax credit): all these figures will be shown on the tax voucher which accompanies the dividend (see page 48). A record of this kind is useful as a check that you have received the dividends, to watch whether dividends are growing, and to fill in your tax return.

Records of your portfolio

From time to time – say, twice a year – you should check on how the performance of your shares has compared with shares as a whole. You do this by calculating the percentage rise (or fall) in the value of all your shares over the period, and comparing this with the rise (or fall) over the same period in a published index of shares. Assuming that most of your shares are those of UK companies, your choice of share index could be:

- The *Financial Times* Industrial Ordinary Share Index. But this is based on only 30 leading industrial companies – and is not representative of UK companies as a whole
- The *Financial Times*/Stock Exchange 100 Index – an index of the 100 largest UK companies, and now the most widely used index

Laserwear plc (25p shares)

	DETAILS OF SHARES BOUGHT...					AND OF THEIR SALE				
A date	B number of shares bought	C price paid per share (excluding charges) p	D total cost of shares (including all charges) £	E share certificate received?	F dates/details of scrip and rights issues	G date	H number of shares sold	J proceeds (after all charges) £	K GAIN (J–D) £	L or LOSS (D–J) £
8/6/87	2,000 1,250	100p	2,177.22 1,357.01	✓	sold	15/10/87	1,250	1,574.17	231.16	
8/6/87	750	106p	814.21							

Example of company-by-company records.

company	number of shares	share price on 30/4/87	valuation on 30/4/87	share price on 28/4/88	valuation on 28/4/88	change over year
East plc	1,700	120p	£2,040	84p	£1,428	−30%
North plc	1,500	187p	£2,805	199p	£2,985	+6.4%
South plc	560	345p	£1,932	402p	£2,251	+16.5%
West plc	776	298p	£2,312	192p	£1,490	−35.5%
TOTAL			£9,089		£8,154	−10.3%
SHARE INDEX[1]		1023.6		928.3		−9.3%

[1]*Financial Times*-Actuaries All-Share Index

Checking on how your shares' performance compares with shares as a whole. Your conclusion is that, although your shares fell in value by 10.3 per cent during the 12-month period, this was only slightly worse than the 9.3 per cent fall in the All-Share Index. You decide to soldier on – and to make the next check on performance in six months' time.

- Or – and the most representative – the *Financial Times*-Actuaries All-Share Index, which is based on the shares of more than 700 companies and is the best guide to the UK share market as a whole.

The first two indexes are widely quoted in the press; but you will probably have to look up the *Financial Times*-Actuaries All-Share Index in the *Financial Times* (mid-month figures are also published from time to time in *Which?*).

On page 111 we give an example of how the comparison can be done. Incidentally, the work of making regular comparisons becomes very much less laborious if you have a computer with a spreadsheet program.

If you own shares in very few companies, you may find that you are getting results which are much better – or much worse – than the market average. If you own shares in a large number of different companies, the chances are that your shares will produce results which are pretty close to the market average.

If you find that your portfolio of shares consistently produces results *better* than shares as a whole (something that is extraordinarily difficult to achieve, as explained in Chapter 10) you will of course be encouraged to continue as your own investment manager. And, similarly, even if the results are only average, but you enjoy making your own investment decisions, you will want to go on doing so.

But what if you find that your portfolio usually does worse than shares as a whole, that your selection of a share is all too often a kiss of death, and/ or that you do not much enjoy the task of buying and selling and keeping detailed records? You may at some point decide that enough is enough, and abdicate in favour of professional management and a quieter life.

Section IV

Next steps

18 *Other share markets*

The Unlisted Securities Market (USM)

This was started by the Stock Exchange in November 1980 as a half-way house between a full Stock Exchange listing (see page 25) and the Over-The-Counter Market (see page 114).

In the past eight years the USM has become quite well established, and nearly 400 companies currently have their shares listed there, including some familiar names like Sock Shop and Pineapple Group. The requirements for getting a USM listing are less stringent than for a full Stock Exchange listing, but companies don't always choose it purely because they can't get a full listing. For example, a company needs to sell only ten per cent of the total value of its shares to the public (whereas a full listing requires 25 per cent) and some companies prefer this – particularly those run by young-ish entrepreneurs who want to keep control over the companies they've built up. The other main requirements for a USM listing are:

- The company must have at least three years' trading record.
- There's no minimum market capitalisation (see page 25), although most companies on the USM have a capitalisation of around £2 million.

Buying and selling
You do this in exactly the same way as for shares with a full listing – with the exception that USM shares may not be so easily marketable, and the spread between the bid and offer prices therefore may be wider.

How safe?

Investments in the USM must be viewed as more risky than buying shares with a full Stock Exchange listing. Some USM companies have provided investors with good returns, and over the years since it began more than 15 per cent of companies have transferred from the USM to a full Stock Exchange listing. However, the fewer restrictions on listing mean that USM companies will generally be smaller, younger, and more speculative. You are covered by the compensation fund set up under the Financial Services Act, e.g. if your broker goes bust (see Chapter 7).

The Third Market

This is the baby of the three markets linked to the Stock Exchange and the most risky of them all. Started in January 1987 for even newer and smaller companies than the USM, requirements for joining are:

● Incorporation in the United Kingdom
● A minimum of *either* one year's audited accounts *or* a fully researched business plan which is expected to generate business during the following year
● At least two brokers have to be prepared to act as market-makers for each company's shares.

You are covered by the compensation scheme set up under the Financial Services Act.

Buying and selling

Again as listed shares, but since at present Third Market shares are classed as delta shares (see Chapter 5) firm prices are not shown on SEAQ.

How safe?

The Third Market has yet to take off, and at the time of writing included shares in only 37 companies. The same reservations apply as for the USM, only more strongly – the companies have practically *no* track record. Only for addicts.

The Over-The-Counter Market (OTC)

A rather nebulous 'market', outside the Stock Exchange market-places, and run by share dealers. There are no requirements for companies to meet before their shares are traded on this market, so the companies involved may be even smaller, younger and riskier than those on the Third Market.

Buying and selling

This usually involves going directly to the market-maker rather than via an agent such as a stockbroker (see page 14). Instead of charging commission, dealers in the OTC market may make their living by selling for a higher price than the price at which they buy. These so-called 'commission-free' deals can therefore work out quite expensive. The other problem is that there may only be one dealer buying and selling the shares – and you may end up with shares you cannot sell.

How safe?

Not at all. Quite apart from the extra riskiness of shares traded on the OTC, in recent months several share dealers have closed down, owing clients money. However, all share dealers must now be 'authorised' under the Financial Services Act, and are therefore covered by a compensation fund (unless they have only interim authorisation – see Chapter 7).

The Business Expansion Scheme (BES)

This was set up to encourage investment in new and possibly risky ventures. By definition, therefore, it's not worthwhile unless you're investing money you're prepared to lose. The attraction of the scheme is the generous tax incentives. Under the scheme, you get tax relief on what you invest in shares in a company not quoted on *either* the Stock Exchange *or* the Unlisted Securities Market (but it can be listed on the Third Market).

Choice of investment

You can invest either directly in individual companies, or in a fund which spreads your money among several BES companies.

If you choose to invest directly in a company, the minimum you can invest is £500 in each company, and for you to get tax relief the company has to be able to provide you with a certificate stating that certain conditions have been met. Only certain companies qualify – *not*:

- Your own company, or one in which you (or your family or business partners) own more than 30 per cent of the business
- A company of which you are a paid director or employee
- Companies incorporated outside the UK
- Companies that have been trading for less than four years
- Companies whose business is in various areas – e.g. farming, banking, insurance, leasing or hiring, share-dealing, accountancy or legal services,

holding collectable goods, investing mainly in property or land (except private rented housing).

If you prefer to invest in a special BES fund, you again have to choose: this time between either 'approved' or 'non-approved' funds. The difference lies in the minimum investment: you need to invest £2,000 in an approved fund (but there's no minimum on the amount in each company in the fund), while you must invest £500 per company in a non-approved fund. The advantage of going for a fund is that they sift through the huge number of companies and select some for you. The disadvantage is that most funds charge an initial fee of say, seven per cent of your investment (which doesn't qualify for tax relief) and some funds also charge a yearly fee of around one per cent.

Getting tax relief

You can get tax relief at your top rate of tax on an investment of up to £40,000 in one tax year (husband and wife count as one person), providing you invest for at least five years. You lose tax relief if the company breaks BES rules within three years, for example by changing its business or getting a quotation on the USM. From 5 April 1987 if you invest in the first half of the tax year – between 6 April and 6 October – you can claim tax relief on up to half of the investment in the previous year. The maximum amount you can carry back in this way is £5,000.

Should you invest?

BES companies have all the drawbacks of other companies not quoted on the Stock Exchange or Unlisted Securities Market, and really the major advantage is the tax relief. So only invest if you're a taxpayer (preferably at the higher rate) prepared to take a risk in return for saving tax. You can get more information from Inland Revenue leaflet IR51 – from local tax and PAYE Enquiry offices.

Investing overseas

As explained in Chapter 8, investing some of your money overseas is a sensible way of reducing risks. You may also want to invest overseas if you believe that the prospects for certain overseas shares, or certain overseas markets, are particularly good.

At present, there are no Exchange Control restrictions on investing overseas, and it is simple enough to place a buying order with a stockbroker – who may either buy the shares himself (if the company is one of the several hundred foreign companies with a quotation on the London Stock Exchange) or arrange to do so via a broker overseas. But unless you are a large-scale investor (with £10,000 or preferably much more to invest at a time) *and* are knowledgeable about overseas share-buying (or have an investment adviser who is), direct investment in overseas shares is not a practical proposition.

Here are some of the problems you would be likely to face:

● Heavy buying and selling costs – an overseas transaction charge (per deal) of perhaps £75 on top of commission; or possibly a lower transaction charge at the outset but additional charges on the payment of each dividend.

● Many US shares are in large denominations (the equivalent of £100 per share, for example), and you probably need to buy 100 shares to have a marketable quantity – so could be facing an outlay of £10,000.

● Japanese shares normally have to be traded in lots of 1,000 shares; and when you get a scrip issue of shares (very common with Japanese shares) you may not be able to sell them except in round numbers of 1,000 shares.

● Administrative problems abound: it is generally best to have the share certificate held by a bank overseas (referred to as an overseas depot), so that the certificate is available for when you want to sell – and arrangements have to be made for this; there can be problems over the name in which the shares are bought, and over tax on the dividends.

● While charges may be less if the shares are those of an overseas company whose shares are traded in London, most of the other complications remain.

So for most people it is very much better to invest overseas by buying the shares of an investment trust company, or units in a unit trust, which specialises in overseas investment. There is a wide choice of both, and it is a matter of choosing an investment trust company or unit trust which invests in the countries – or in the selection of countries – that you want.

Before you invest, make a point of finding out what the investment policy is. Do not choose simply on the basis of which countries' shares are currently held by the investment trust company or unit trust, because this might change in a way you do not want. There are other points to watch, too. Investment trust company shares may fluctuate in value more than unit trusts – and tend to do well in good times for shares, rather badly in lean times. And watch out for management charges – generally lower with investment trust companies. Annual management charges on unit trusts, by contrast, are becoming rather steep – 1.5 per cent of the value of your investment is now quite common, with some unit trusts charging 2 per cent.

For information about investment trust companies, see *The Investment Trust Year Book* (try your local business or university library). Monthly statistics are published in the *Financial Times* and *Daily Telegraph* on the fourth Saturday in the month.

For information about unit trusts, try your local library for the *Unit Trust Year Book*, or one of the monthly magazines dealing with unit trusts – *Money Management*, *Planned Savings*, or *Unit Trust Management*.

19 *Options*

In effect, someone who invests in **options** is staking his money on whether the price of a particular share is going to rise, or fall, during the following few months – and by how much. Since it is impossible for anyone to know what will happen to share prices in the future, options amount to a form of gambling. And, in the grand tradition of most higher forms of gambling, options can be complicated, high risk – and rewarding to those who are running them. But although options are inherently high risk, they can be used to *reduce* the overall risk to which an investor is exposed.

There are two basic types: *non-traded (or traditional) options* and *traded options*. We will look at non-traded options first: the original type, now less common – but relatively simple, and a good introduction to the extra complications of traded options.

Non-traded (traditional) options

A **call option** gives the holder the right to buy – within a stated period of time – a given number of shares in a given company at a fixed price (called the *exercise price* or *striking price*) which will be at the offer price of the shares at the time the call option is taken out. The option would usually cost around 5 to 15 per cent of the share price at the time the option was taken out. There are also commission charges (plus VAT) which you usually pay at the time of taking out the option. These charges are generally at the same rates as those for buying shares but are calculated on the exercise price – not on the price of the option. So commission charges are large in relation to your outlay. You will also be liable for Stamp Duty – at the normal rate of 0.5 per cent – if you exercise your option to buy the shares; Stamp Duty is not charged until the time that you exercise your option.

The normal option period is three months, and the holder can exercise the option at any time during the three months. If you do not exercise the option during that period – because the share price has not risen enough to make it worthwhile doing so – the option lapses, and you have lost the money you spent on buying it. As consolation, however, your loss counts as a loss for capital gains tax (see Chapter 6).

A call option is the kind to buy if you are confident that the share price of that company is going to rise during the next three months, and you wish to gamble on your hunch. In this situation you could, instead, buy the shares rather than take out a call option – but the percentage gain can be very much greater with an option. Of course, you can have absolutely no grounds for confidence that the shares will rise: it is not possible to predict the long-term performance of a company's shares (see Chapter 10), let alone the short-term performance, other than by the use of inside information (which would be a criminal offence to profit from).

A call option is the most usual kind of non-traded option but is not the only one. There is also a **put option**, which is exactly the opposite of a call option. A put option gives the holder of the option a right to *sell* shares at the exercise price – and is for an investor who is confident that the share price is going to fall. The costs, and risks, are broadly the same as for a call option, the difference being that the investor stands to gain if the share price falls and to lose if the share price rises.

For investors who feel sure that a company's shares are on the move – but do not profess to know whether the price will go up or down – there is a *double option*. This might be worth considering, for instance, during a takeover bid – at a time of uncertainty when, if the bid were to go through, the share price would certainly rise, but if it were withdrawn and no other bidder emerged, the price could well fall. A double option gives its holder the right to buy shares if the share price rises *or* sell shares if the share price falls (though not both at the same time, of course). But a double option is expensive – double the cost of a call or put option. And the catch is that if the share price does not rise enough (or fall enough) to make it worthwhile exercising your right to buy (or sell), the option will lapse and you will lose your money. And you will have lost double the amount that a call or a put option would have lost you.

With non-traded options it is only possible to arrange a call option (say) if there is someone else – in practice, usually an institutional investor – who is willing to accept the option money and undertake to sell shares at the exercise price. Or, with a put option, the converse – an investor who will accept the option money and undertake to buy shares at the exercise price. Although not normally difficult to arrange, non-traded options lacked the flexibility that a market could provide – and this has led to the introduction of *traded options*.

Example

You are confident that the shares of Multignome – now standing at 240p – are going to rise sharply during the following three months, and have around £2,000 available to back your fancy. A three-month call option price is 24p, with an exercise price of 240p.

We will suppose, first, that you are proved right, and that the shares rise to 290p. This is how you would have fared:

- If you had spent £2,000 on buying shares in Multignome you could have bought around 830 shares – and since the share price rose from 240p to 290p, you could have made a profit of around 50p per share – i.e. a profit of around £415 (less expenses).
- At the other extreme, if you had spent £2,000 on buying call options in Multignome you could have bought options on more than 8,300 shares, and if you exercised these when the share price had risen to 290p you could have made a profit of some 50p per share – by buying the shares for 240p and immediately selling them for 290p – from which profit you must deduct the 24p per share cost of the options. So your net profit would be some 26p per share, i.e. a profit of around £2,160 (less expenses).
- Or you could have steered some middle course, by buying a smaller number of options on Multignome shares and putting the balance of your money in something very much less risky (such as a building society). This would of course reduce the risk, and also your gain.

But now look at the other side of the coin. Suppose that, despite your confident belief that the share price would rise, Multignome shares actually fell from 240p to 190p:

- If you had spent £2,000 on buying some 830 Multignome shares at 240p, the value of your investment would have fallen to around £1,580 – so you would be showing a loss of around £420. Of course, you would not necessarily have to sell the shares and incur this loss – you could continue to hold the shares in the hope that better days would return.
- If you had spent £2,000 on buying call options in Multignome, you would not have been able to exercise the options – and they would have lapsed. So you would have a loss of £2,000 (plus expenses).
- If you had spent less than £2,000 – say £1,000 – on buying call options, you would have a loss of £1,000, and this would be further reduced by the interest earned by the balance of your money in, say, a building society.

To sum up. In this example, where the Multignome share price moved up – or down – by around 20 per cent, the result of investing £2,000 in the shares could be a gain – or loss – of some £400. By contrast, by buying call options you could gain – or lose – some £2,000.

Traded options

The London Traded Options Market started business in 1978, closely modelled on American traded options markets. Traded options are – like the non-traded kind – high risk; they are also extremely complex and suitable only for advanced investors who will also take the trouble to follow the market carefully. In this book we give a brief outline of what is involved; for more information, write to the Stock Exchange for booklets produced by their Options Development Group. For a book on the subject, there is *Trading in Options* by Geoffrey Chamberlain, published by Woodhead-Faulkner. Not all stockbrokers deal in traded options: ask the Stock Exchange for a list of those who do, and who are willing to take on new private clients.

A traded option takes the form of a call or a put option, with the main difference that it can be traded (bought and sold) during its life. So an investor in traded options can exercise the option – i.e. buy or sell the relevant shares at the exercise price – or he can sell the option for what it will fetch in the market.

Currently, traded options are available on some 60 UK shares, all of them leading alpha stocks. Traded options are also available on a share index (the *Financial Times*/Stock Exchange 100 Index), three government stocks, and South African mining shares.

With traded options, a contract – which is the unit which you buy or sell – usually represents 1,000 shares, and you can deal in any number of contracts. When a series of options is created for a share for the first time, it will include options with expiry dates fixed at three, six and nine months ahead. When the first expiry date is reached – in three months' time – a new expiry date is created, so that there will always be three expiry dates at intervals of three months. Options with up to three different exercise prices will be created; and if the actual share price rises above the highest exercise price – or below the lowest – more options will be created. So at any one time there may be three or four or more exercise prices for any one share – see the example of traded options prices (from the *Financial Times*), opposite.

When buying a traded option, you have quite a list of decisions to make: whether you want a call or a put option, what expiry date you want (there will always be three to choose from, spaced at three-monthly intervals), and what exercise price you want (from a range of three up to perhaps six.)

Note that the market price of a traded option can have two parts. If it is a call option and the current share price is *higher* than the exercise price, the traded option has an *intrinsic value* which is in fact the difference between the share price and the exercise price (conversely, if the share price is *lower*

LONDON TRADED OPTIONS

Option		CALLS			PUTS			Option		CALLS			PUTS		
		July	Oct.	Jan.	July	Oct.	Jan.			Aug.	Nov.	Feb.	Aug.	Nov.	Feb.
Allied Lyons (*429)	390	43	60	70	2	10	15	Guinness (*363)	300	68	73	—	2	5	—
	420	18	42	53	7	20	25		330	40	55	68	5	12	16
	460	4	21	33	35	42	48		360	20	37	48	13	23	28
									390	8	25	38	33	38	45
Brit. Airways (*147)	130	19	28	--	2	8	—	Ladbroke (*419)	403	35	44	—	12	17	—
	140	9	20	29	6	12	18		420	—	—	45	—	—	30
	160	3	10	19	20	23	28		443	13	25	—	30	38	—
British Gas (*178)	165	15	23	30	1¼	7	11	LASMO (*320)	260	63	74	846	2	9	12
	180	4	12	23	7½	14	18		280	45	60	73	4	13	19
	200	0½	3	15	24	29	33		300	29	43	57	9	17	24
									330	13½	26	37	20	27	30
B.P. (*389)	330	62	72	79	2	6	12	P. & O. (*742)	638	113	123	143	3	10	10
	360	35	50	63	6	16	21		688	67	88	113	5	18	25
	390	15	31	47	16	27	35		750	25	50	72	30	42	50
Britoil (*311)	240	75	80	87	2	4	9	Plessey (*227)	200	33	40	48	4	8	9
	260	55	61	69	2	5	12		220	19	28	34	12	16	18
	280	38	49	58	3	10	18		240	10	19	24	22	26	30
	300	23	37	44	7	17	27								

Part of London Traded Options prices from the *Financial Times*

than the exercise price, the traded option has no intrinsic value). If it is a put option, the intrinsic value (if any) is the amount by which the current share price is *lower* than the exercise price. With both call and put options, the remainder of the price is the *time value* – and the further away the expiry date, the higher this time value will be.

Look, for example, at the prices for traded options on Allied Lyons shares, above. On the date the prices relate to, the actual share price was 429p (first column). Call options would have cost between 4p and 70p per share – the lower the exercise price (second column) and the further away the expiry date, the higher the price of the option. Put options would have cost between 2p and 48p per share – and here the higher the exercise price and further away the expiry date, the higher the price of the option.

The strategies of option-buying are complex, and outside the scope of this book. In general, the most speculative traded options are those with no intrinsic value at all. Those with a substantial intrinsic value are less speculative. And it is possible to use options to reduce the overall level of risk in your portfolio of shares.

Warrants

Some companies (particularly investment trust companies) have issued *warrants*. These give the holder the right to buy shares in the company concerned at a set price, at a set time (or times) in the future – in some cases, years ahead. So warrants are in effect long-term options, which are bought and sold on the Stock Exchange (whereas traded options have their own, separate, market place).

Warrant holders get no dividends, and have no voting rights – but (as with options) stand to make larger gains if the share price rises than they would by investing the same amount of money directly in the company's shares. Conversely, warrant holders stand to make larger losses if the share price falls.

Glossary

Note: **bold** is used for each Glossary entry; *italics* for terms defined within an entry (but without an entry of their own); SMALL CAPITALS for terms that have their own entry elsewhere in the Glossary

'A' shares Usually, ordinary shares without voting rights. Price often lower than the equivalent vote-carrying ordinary shares.

Account The Stock Exchange year is divided up into accounts (around 24 of them). Each account normally lasts ten working days – starting on a Monday and ending on the Friday of the following week. At the end of each account, each investor's purchases and sales of shares are totted up, and the balance becomes due from him (or is owed to him) on SETTLEMENT DAY.

Account day Another name for SETTLEMENT DAY.

After-hours trading After the Stock Exchange has officially closed (now 5pm). Trading goes on, but most deals count as the next day's business (called *early bargains*).

Alpha stocks Shares of some 100 of the largest and most widely traded companies.

At best The lowest buying price – or the highest selling price – that the broker can find.

Bargain Not necessarily. Simply means a deal to buy or sell shares.

Bear Someone who believes that a particular share, or the market, is going to fall.

Bear market Period of time – more usually months than years – when most share prices fall, and pessimism prevails.

Beta Or *beta coefficient*. A measure of a share's propensity to rise (or fall) in price as the share market as a whole rises (or falls). No connection with BETA STOCKS.

Beta stocks The shares of some 600 companies, the next category down from the ALPHA STOCKS.

Bid price Price which a seller of shares receives.

Blue chip Large and well-established company.

Bonus issue See SCRIP ISSUE.

British Government stocks Securities issued and guaranteed by the government.

Broker Someone who acts as your agent when buying and selling shares, and may offer advice.

Broker-dealer Official name for stockbroker.

Bull Someone who believes that a particular share, or the market, is going to rise.

Bull market Period of time – months or years – when most share prices rise, and optimism prevails.

Call Payment due, e.g. instalment on PARTLY PAID shares.

Call option An OPTION which gives the right to buy shares at a fixed price.

Capitalisation issue See SCRIP ISSUE.

Cash settlement Payment straight away – not at next SETTLEMENT DAY.

Chartism Same as TECHNICAL ANALYSIS.

Chinese walls Built between, say, the broking and the share-issuing parts of a financial conglomerate to try to ensure that one does not influence the other.

Choice price When highest

BID PRICE = lowest OFFER PRICE.

Churning Excessive buying and selling of shares by an investment manager, mainly to earn commission.

Closing commission If you buy shares and sell them again during the same Stock Exchange account, the second deal should be subject to closing commission (which should be nil). The same applies if you sell shares which you do not have, in order to buy them back later in the account at (you hope) a lower price – something for advanced investors only.

Closing prices Prices at 5pm (official Stock Exchange closing time). Prices printed in newspapers usually relate to around (not necessarily at) this time.

Consideration What you pay for shares when buying (or receive when selling), exclusive of any charges.

Contract note Confirmation from stockbroker that he has bought or sold shares – with full details and prices. Must be time-stamped, or say that this information is available, and must say if the shares have been bought from (or sold to) the market-making arm of the stockbroker.

Cum Latin for 'with'. For example, if you buy shares *cum dividend* you are entitled to the next dividend.

Dealer Someone who buys shares and holds them for resale, hoping to make a profit.

Debentures Fixed-income investments.

Delta stocks Shares of the least actively traded companies on the Stock Exchange.

Discount With NEW ISSUES: amount by which the market price is below the issue price. Also applies to INVESTMENT TRUST COMPANY shares, which are said to trade at a discount when the market price of the shares is below the NET ASSET VALUE per share.

Discretionary The stockbroker takes the investment decisions (not you).

Dividend The amount per share paid out by the company from its profits. Companies usually pay dividends twice a year (though if in difficulties, may pay no dividend at all). A smaller amount – the *interim dividend* – is usually paid in the middle of the company's financial year. At the end of the financial year, the company will normally pay a larger amount, the *final dividend*. The two payments added together are called the *total dividend for the year* – or simply the dividend. The investor receives dividends net of the equivalent of basic-rate tax, along with a tax credit. *Gross dividend* is dividend + tax credit; *net dividend* is without the tax credit.

Dividend cover How many times the total dividend for the year could have been paid out of the company's after-tax profits for the year.

Dividend yield Income from each £100 invested.

Earnings per share After-tax profits of a company due to its ordinary shareholders, calculated on a per-share basis.

Efficient Market Hypothesis This comes in three versions. Overwhelming evidence for the *Weak Form* – which states that current share prices fully reflect all that can be known from a study of the past peformance of the shares and volume of shares sold. It is therefore useless to select shares on the basis of past performance (and useless to rely on TECHNICAL ANALYSIS). Good evidence for the *Semi-strong Form*, which states that current share prices fully reflect all publicly available information about the companies. So it is useless to select shares on the basis of such information. Not such convincing evidence for the *Strong Form*, which states that current share prices fully reflect *all* information about the companies (not just publicly available information). For some small overseas stock markets, the Efficient Market Hypothesis may not always apply.

Equities Another word for ORDINARY SHARES.

Ex Latin for 'without'. See under XC, XD, XR.

Execution-only Share dealing service which does not offer the investor any advice.

Exercise price The fixed price at which, with a CALL OPTION, you have the right to buy shares (or, with a PUT OPTION, to sell them).

Flotation see NEW ISSUE.

Free issue see SCRIP ISSUE.

Financial Times-Actuaries Share Indexes Series of indexes of shares in different sectors of the market. The *All-Share Index* combines all these into an index of the shares of more than 700 companies – the best guide to the UK share market as a whole.

Financial Times Industrial Ordinary Share Index Index of 30 leading industrial shares. Not representative of UK shares as a whole.

Financial Times/Stock Exchange 100 Index Or *Footsie*. Index of the 100 largest UK companies. Its special feature: recalculated minute by minute. Now the most widely used index for UK shares.

Form of renunciation Form printed on LETTER OF ALLOTMENT, which you complete to sell the shares or transfer them to another name.

Fundamental analysis Study of companies' earnings and prospects, in order to assess the value of their shares.

Gamma stocks Shares of some 1,700 companies – less actively traded than BETA STOCKS but more so than DELTA STOCKS.

Growth stocks Shares which do better than the market as a whole, for many years.

Hedge Buying one type of investment in the hope of counteracting possible losses on another.

Insider trading Or *insider dealing*. Using privileged information about a company to buy or sell its shares. A criminal offence.

Investment trust company A company in the business of investing in other companies' shares.

Issuing house Company responsible for marketing NEW ISSUES.

Letter of allotment Confirmation of how many NEW ISSUE shares you have succeeded in buying. Also called *letter of acceptance*.

Limit Instructions to a stockbroker to buy (or sell) at a fixed price or better.

Listed company Or *fully listed* company, or company with *full listing*. One whose shares are traded on the Stock Exchange.

Loan stock Fixed-income investments.

Market-maker SEE DEALER.

Middle-market price Or *middle price*. Calculated price, half way between the BID PRICE and OFFER PRICE.

Net asset value (NAV) Amount by which the assets of a company exceed its liabilities, worked out as pence per share.

New issue Shares of a company coming to the market for the first time.

New shares Shares which can be transferred by a FORM OF RENUNCIATION.

Nil-paid rights Your rights to extra shares under a RIGHTS ISSUE which you have not (yet) taken up. They normally have a value: the EX-RIGHTS price of the shares, minus the price at which the rights have been offered.

Nominal value Shares of UK companies are given a nominal value (often 25p). Of virtually no importance to the investor. Some companies still use the nominal value, however, as a basis for expressing the amount of their dividends: for example, if a company declares a dividend of 20 per cent, and if the nominal value of its shares is 20p, the dividend is 4p per share.

Nominee Shares are commonly registered in a nominee name (instead of your own) if they are managed for you.

Offer for sale Offer of NEW ISSUE shares at a fixed price.

Offer for sale by tender Offer of NEW ISSUE shares where the investor names the price he is willing to pay.

Offer price Price which a buyer of shares pays.

Opening prices Prices at 9am (official Stock Exchange opening time).

Option The right to buy (or sell) shares at a fixed price within a set number of months. For advanced investors.

Ordinary shares What is normally meant by the word 'shares'. When you buy ordinary shares you are literally buying a share in the company, with a right to receive the dividend (if any), and a right to vote (unless they're non-voting 'A' SHARES).

Over-The-Counter Market (OTC) Market in shares of very small companies, run by dealers.

Oversubscribed More applications for a NEW ISSUE than there are shares available.

Par value Same as NOMINAL VALUE.

Partly paid Full cost of share not yet paid – future instalments due.

Penny shares Share price under 50p. Often high risk: could be a bargain – or an out-and-out loser.

Personal Equity Plans (PEPs) Share-buying scheme with tax relief – but with pitfalls, too.

Portfolio The set of different investments (particularly shares) owned by one person.

Preference shares More like fixed income investments than shares. Receive fixed dividends (if the money is there) – and they take priority over ordinary shares.

Premium Particularly with NEW ISSUES: amount by which the market price exceeds the issue price. May also apply to INVESTMENT TRUST COMPANY shares, which are said to trade at a premium in the (rather rare) cases when the market price of the shares exceeds the NET ASSET VALUE per share.

Price/earnings ratio (P/E or PE) The current share price divided by the EARNINGS PER SHARE.

Primary market NEW ISSUES and RIGHTS ISSUES.

Prior charges Interest and dividends which have to be paid to holders of fixed income investments and preference shares before dividends can be paid to the company's ordinary shareholders.

Privatisation Sale of shares in nationalised industries.

Prospectus Document with detailed information about a company, required before any NEW ISSUE of shares can be made.

Public limited company (plc) Only public limited companies – not private ones – can issue shares to the public.

Put option An OPTION which gives the right to sell shares at a fixed price.

Quotation suspended Official listing has been temporarily withdrawn, and no dealings are allowed.

Quoted company See LISTED COMPANY.

Random walk theory Says that the past price record of a company's shares cannot be used for predicting future price movements.

Rights issue Allotment of extra shares to shareholders in proportion to their existing shareholding – at a fixed price.

SAEF (SEAQ Automatic Execution Facility) Future computer system which will allow automatic deals at TOUCH prices via SEAQ.

SEAQ (Stock Exchange Automated Quotation System) Computer system for quoting firm BID and OFFER PRICES from different MARKET-MAKERS, and recording deals.

Scrip issue Issue of extra shares to shareholders in proportion to their existing shareholding – no payment involved.

Secondary market Trading in shares after they have been issued i.e. any trading in shares other than NEW ISSUES or RIGHTS ISSUES.

Securities STOCKS and SHARES.

Settlement day The day when all deals made in the last Stock Exchange account must be settled. Normally on a Monday, ten days after the end of the account.

Share certificate Official document showing how many shares you own.

Shares Usually means ORDINARY SHARES.

Spread The gap between the BID and OFFER prices.

Stag Someone who applies for NEW ISSUES in the hope of making a quick sale at a profit.

Stocks Main meaning: fixed income investments (e.g. British Government stocks). But also a general term for stocks *and* shares (as in the STOCK EXCHANGE) or can simply mean shares (as in ALPHA STOCKS).

Stockbroker Member of the STOCK EXCHANGE. Now officially called BROKER-DEALERS: many firms combine roles of BROKER and DEALER.

Stock Exchange Market-place for stocks and shares. Full title of what is referred to as 'The Stock Exchange' is *The International Stock Exchange of the United Kingdom and the Republic of Ireland*. The Self-Regulating Organisation for the Stock Exchange is *The Securities Association (TSA)*.

Striking price Price at which shares are allocated under an OFFER FOR SALE BY TENDER. Also another term for EXERCISE PRICE.

TALISMAN (Transfer Accounting Lodgement for Investors, Stock MANagement for jobbers) The Stock Exchange's computerised settlement system. (Jobbers are extinct – replaced by MARKET-MAKERS.)

TAURUS (Transfer and AUtomated Registration of Uncertificated Stock) Future Stock Exchange computer system, which will 'dematerialise' SHARE CERTIFICATES.

Technical analysis Study of charts of past share prices in order to decide when to buy and sell a company's shares.

Third Market The Stock Exchange's market (to compete with OVER-THE-COUNTER MARKET) for small companies which do not qualify for the UNLISTED SECURITIES MARKET or FULL LISTING.

TOPIC (Teletext Output of Price Information by Computer) The Stock Exchange's screen-based price and information system. Now carries SEAQ prices, as well as middle-market prices for non-SEAQ shares and other financial information.

Touch The highest BID and lowest OFFER price available for any share.

Traded option An OPTION which can be traded (bought and sold) during its life on the Traded Options Market. For advanced investors.

Transfer form Also *transfer deed*. What you must sign after selling shares.

Undersubscribed More NEW ISSUE shares available than there are applications to buy. Bad news for STAGS.

Unit trust A trust fund – in most cases, predominantly of shares – divided into a large number of units. Investors can buy and sell units at prices set by the unit trust managers: the prices must be based on the market value of the investments in the fund, adjusted for charges.

Unlisted Securities Market (USM) Market run by the Stock Exchange for (mainly) smaller and younger companies which do not qualify for – or do not want – a full Stock Exchange listing.

Warrant In effect, a long-term OPTION to buy shares at a set price (often over a period of several years). For advanced investors.

xc Ex-capitalisation or ex-scrip (means the same). The share price has been adjusted (downwards) to take account of the scrip issue.

xd Ex-dividend. The buyer of the shares won't get the next DIVIDEND which has been declared and is due to be paid.

xr Ex-rights. The share price has been adjusted (downwards) to take account of the RIGHTS ISSUE.

yield see DIVIDEND YIELD.

Useful addresses

For further general information, any specific enquiry or complaint, contact the relevant organisation below. Many also issue their own publications on stocks and shares.

General information

THE INTERNATIONAL STOCK EXCHANGE OF GREAT BRITAIN AND THE REPUBLIC OF IRELAND LTD

(Public Affairs Department)
Old Broad Street
London EC2N 1HP
Tel: 01-588 2355

(Publications)
4th Floor
50 Finsbury Square
London EC2A 1DD
Tel: 01-588 2355

REGIONAL STOCK EXCHANGES

Belfast
Northern House
10 High Street
Belfast
BT1 2BP
Tel: 0232 321094

Birmingham
Margaret Street
Birmingham
B3 3JL
Tel: 021-236 9181

Bristol
St Nicholas Street
Bristol
BS1 1TH
Tel: 0272 264541

Dublin
28 Anglesea Street
Dublin 2
Republic of Ireland
Tel: 0001 778808

Glasgow
7 Nelson Mandela Place
PO Box 141
Glasgow
G2 1BU
Tel: 041-221 7060

Leeds
Royal Exchange House
City Square
Leeds
LS1 5SG
Tel: 0532 451511

Liverpool
Silkhouse Court
Tithebarn Street
Liverpool
L2 2LT
Tel: 051-236 0869

Manchester
76 King Street
Manchester
M2 4NH
Tel: 061-833 0931

Newcastle
Commercial Union House
39 Pilgrim's Street
Newcastle-upon-Tyne
NE1 6RJ
Tel: 091-232 7355

NATIONAL ASSOCIATION OF INVESTMENT CLUBS

c/o Chadwick & Co
Halifax House
5 Fenwick Street
Liverpool L2 0PR
Tel: 051-236 6262

WIDER SHARE OWNERSHIP COUNCIL

Juxon House
94 St Paul's Churchyard
London EC4M 8EH
Tel: 01-248 9155

British Government stocks

BANK OF ENGLAND

Registrars' Department
– Stock Enquiries
New Change
Watling Street
London EC4M 9AA
Tel: 01-601 4444

BONDS AND STOCK OFFICE

(for enquiries about government stocks bought on the National Savings Stock Register)
Preston New Road
Blackpool
Lancashire
FY3 9YP
Tel: 0253 697333

NATIONAL SAVINGS
CERTIFICATE AND
SAYE OFFICE

Milburngate House
Durham
DH99 1NS
Tel: 091-386 4900

DEPARTMENT OF
NATIONAL SAVINGS

(also for information on
National Savings)
Headquarters Unit
Charles House
375 Kensington High
Street
London
W14 8SD
Tel: 01-605 9461

Company information

COMPANIES'
REGISTRATION
OFFICE

London
Department of Trade
Companies House
55–71 City Road
London
EC1Y 1BB
Tel: 01-253 9393

Belfast
IDB House
Companies Registry
64 Chichester Street
Belfast
BT1 4JX
Tel: 0232 234488

Cardiff
Companies Registration
Office
Companies House
Crown Way
Maindy
Cardiff
CF4 3UZ
Tel: 0222 388588

Edinburgh
Companies Registration
Office
102 George Street
Edinburgh
EH2 3DJ
Tel: 031-225 5774

EXTEL FINANCIAL
LTD

37–45 Paul Street
London
EC2A 4BP
Tel: 01-251 0344

PRESTEL –
CITISERVICE

ICV Information
Systems Ltd
Woodstead House
72 Chertsey Road
Woking
Surrey
GU21 5BJ
Tel: 048 62 27431

Complaints

BANKING
OMBUDSMAN
BUREAU

The Office of the
Banking Ombudsman
Citadel House
5–11 Fetter Lane
London
EC4A 1BR
Tel: 01-583 1395

BUILDING SOCIETY
OMBUDSMAN

Grosvenor Gardens
House
35–37 Grosvenor
Gardens
London
SW1X 7AW
Tel: 01-931 0044

INSURANCE
OMBUDSMAN BUREAU
(also covers unit trusts)

31 Southampton Row
London
WC1B 5HJ
Tel: 01-242 8613

Regulating bodies

ASSOCIATION OF
FUTURES BROKERS AND
DEALERS (AFBD)

B Section, 5th Floor
Plantation House
4–16 Mincing Lane
London
EC3M 3DX
Tel: 01-626 9763

DEPARTMENT OF
TRADE AND
INDUSTRY (DTI)

1 Victoria Street
London
SW1H 0ET
Tel: 01-215 7877

FINANCIAL
INTERMEDIARIES,
MANAGERS AND
BROKERS REGULATORY
ASSOCIATION (FIMBRA)

Hertsmere House
Marsh Wall
London
E14 9RW
Tel: 01-538 8860

INVESTMENT
MANAGEMENT
REGULATORY
ORGANISATION (IMRO)

Centre Point
103 New Oxford Street
London
WC1A 1PT
Tel: 01-379 0601

LIFE ASSURANCE
AND UNIT TRUST
REGULATORY
ORGANISATION
(LAUTRO)

Centre Point
103 New Oxford Street
London
WC1A 1QH
Tel: 01-379 0444

MONOPOLIES AND
MERGERS
COMMISSION (MMC)

New Court
48 Carey Street
London
WC2A 2JE
Tel: 01-831 6111

OFFICE OF FAIR
TRADING (OFT)

Field House
15–25 Bream's
Buildings
London
EC4A 1PR
Tel: 01-242 2858

PANEL ON TAKE-
OVERS AND
MERGERS (PTM)

PO Box 226
The Stock Exchange
Building
London
EC2P 2JX
Tel: 01-382 9026

THE SECURITIES
ASSOCIATION (TSA)

The Stock Exchange
Tower
22nd Floor
Old Broad Street
London
EC2N 1HP
Tel: 01-256 9000

SECURITIES AND
INVESTMENTS
BOARD (SIB)

3 Royal Exchange
Buildings
London
EC3V 3NL
Tel: 01-283 2474

Tax information

For income tax and
capital gains tax queries
contact your local Tax
Inspector or PAYE
enquiry office – look in
the phone book under
Inland Revenue for
addresses and telephone
numbers

CAPITAL TAXES
OFFICES

(for inheritance tax
queries)
London
Minford House
Rockley Road
London
W14 0DF
Tel: 01-603 4622

Belfast
Law Court Buildings
Chichester Street
Belfast
BT1 3NU
Tel: 0232 235111

Edinburgh
16 Picardy Place
Edinburgh
EH1 3NB
Tel: 031-556 8511

INLAND REVENUE

Somerset House
The Strand
London
WC2R 1LB
Tel: 01-438 6420

Trade organisations

ASSOCIATION OF
BRITISH INSURERS

Aldermary House
10–15 Queen Street
London
EC4N 1WT
Tel: 01-248 4477

ASSOCIATION OF
INVESTMENT TRUST
COMPANIES

6th Floor
Park House
16 Finsbury Circus
London
EC2M 7JJ
Tel: 01-588 5347

BANKING
INFORMATION
SERVICE

10 Lombard Street
London
EC3V 9AP
Tel: 01-626 8486

BRITISH INSURANCE
AND INVESTMENT
BROKERS'
ASSOCIATION

14 Bevis Marks
London
EC3A 7NT
Tel: 01-623 9043

UNIT TRUST
ASSOCIATION

(Information Unit)
53–54 Haymarket
London
SW1Y 4RP
Tel: 01-930 4241

Index

Unlisted Securities Market, (USM) 25–
    6, 64, 65, 71, 82, 113–4, 129
  PEP 27
unsecured loan stock 11
unsolicited sales calls 56
unused rights 98

variable interest gilts 23
VAT 42, 43, 45, 119

voting rights 11, 103

warrants 124, 130
white knights 93
wife's investment income 47
written customer agreements 56

xd 83, 130

yield 65, 72–3, 76, 84, 126